Out of Space

Out of Space

CREATING SAFE SPACES
IN UNLIKELY PLACES

JULIO C. ROMAN

LIONCREST
PUBLISHING

OUT OF SPACE

Creating Safe Spaces in Unlikely Places

ISBN	978-1-5445-2807-6	*Hardcover*
	978-1-5445-2805-2	*Paperback*
	978-1-5445-2806-9	*Ebook*

Contents

Author's Note

I have received the approval to use many of the names in this book; in other cases, names, events, and minor details may have been changed to protect the identity and privacy of some involved. My accounts are written as I remember living them. When I needed clarity for accuracy, context, and background, I sought those who shared the same space during my experiences to help recollect the tone, attitude, and intensity of the moment.

Trigger warnings (TW) will be used in this book as a notice of upcoming sensitive content, to prevent exposing someone with past trauma to topics that might incite a physical and/or mental reaction (e.g., sexual violence, domestic violence, and death).

This book is dedicated to the forty-nine souls whose lives and safe spaces were taken from them on June 12, 2016, at the Pulse nightclub shooting in Orlando, Florida.

STANLEY ALMODÓVAR III,
23 years old

DEONKA DEIDRA DRAYTON,
32 years old

AMANDA ALVEAR,
25 years old

SIMON ADRIAN CARRILLO FERNÁNDEZ,
31 years old

OSCAR AMBIORIX ARACENA-MONTERO,
26 years old

LEROY VALENTÍN FERNÁNDEZ,
25 years old

RODOLFO AYALA-AYALA,
33 years old

MERCEDEZ MARISOL FLORES,
26 years old

ANTONIO DAVON BROWN,
29 years old

PETER OMMY GONZÁLEZ-CRUZ,
22 years old

DARRYL ROMAN BURT II,
29 years old

JUAN RAMÓN GUERRERO,
22 years old

ANGEL LUIS CANDELARIO-PADRO,
28 years old

PAUL TERRELL HENRY,
41 years old

JUAN CHEVEZ-MARTÍNEZ,
25 years old

FRANK HERNÁNDEZ ESCALANTE,
27 years old

LUIS DANIEL CONDE,
39 years old

MIGUEL ANGEL HONORATO,
30 years old

CORY JAMES CONNELL,
21 years old

JAVIER JORGE-REYES,
40 years old

TEVIN EUGENE CROSBY,
25 years old

JASON BENJAMIN JOSAPHAT,
19 years old

EDDIE JAMOLDROY JUSTICE,
30 years old

JEAN CARLOS NIEVES RODRÍGUEZ,
27 years old

ANTHONY LUIS LAUREANO DISLA,
25 years old

XAVIER EMMANUEL SERRANO ROSADO,
35 years old

CHRISTOPHER ANDREW LEINONEN,
32 years old

CHRISTOPHER JOSEPH SANFELIZ,
24 years old

ALEJANDRO BARRIOS MARTÍNEZ,
21 years old

YILMARY RODRÍGUEZ SOLIVAN,
24 years old

BRENDA LEE MÁRQUEZ MCCOOL,
49 years old

EDWARD MANUEL SOTOMAYOR, JR.,
34 years old

GILBERTO RAMON SILVA MENÉNDEZ,
25 years old

SHANE EVAN TOMLINSON,
33 years old

KIMBERLY MORRIS,
37 years old

MARTIN BENÍTEZ TORRES,
33 years old

AKYRA MONET MURRAY,
18 years old

JONATHAN ANTONIO CAMUY VEGA,
24 years old

LUIS OMAR OCASIO-CAPO,
20 years old

JUAN PABLO RIVERA VELÁZQUEZ,
37 years old

GERALDO ANTONIO ORTIZ-JIMÉNEZ,
25 years old

LUIS SERGIO VIELMA,
22 years old

ERIC IVAN ORTIZ-RIVERA,
36 years old

FRANKY JIMMY DEJESÚS VELÁZQUEZ,
50 years old

JOEL RAYON PANIAGUA,
32 years old

LUIS DANIEL WILSON-LEON,
37 years old

JEAN CARLOS MÉNDEZ PÉREZ,
35 years old

JERALD ARTHUR WRIGHT,
31 years old

ENRIQUE L. RÍOS, JR.,
25 years old

"That nothing here is promised, not one day...
And love is love is love is love is love is love is love is love
cannot be killed or swept aside...
Now fill the world with music, love, and pride."

—LIN-MANUEL MIRANDA

The Pulse of a Community

"Of course, I am afraid, because the transformation of
silence into language and action is an act of self-revelation,
and that always seems fraught with danger."

—AUDRE LORDE, AUTHOR AND ACTIVIST

I wrote this book so that other LGBTQIA+ people may see pieces
of their stories in mine. I wrote it to share leadership lessons I
have collected and learned along the way. This is not meant to be a
holy grail, but a toolbox filled with real-life narratives and advice.

For twenty-two amazing years, I've had the honor of creating
safe spaces for Black and Brown Lesbian, Gay, Bisexual, Transgender, Queer or Questioning, Intersex, Asexual (LGBTQIA+),
and other marginalized communities. This includes advancing
health equality, social justice, and public health initiatives for
these communities. In this book, I share honest pieces of my
story as I navigated life as a queer, timid Latino boy who would
one day become a confident gay man who mentors and advocates
for other LGBTQIA+ leaders. My journey isn't for the faint of
heart, but it is a life lesson in determination. I share experiences
of sexual and physical abuse, homelessness, drug use, sex work,
and HIV and AIDS—but also deep faith, family, forgiveness,
and finding my calling.

The Oxford Dictionary defines *safe space* as: "a place or environment in which a person or category of people can feel confident that they will not be exposed to discrimination, criticism, harassment, or any other emotional or physical harm."

On my safe space journey, I have learned one crucial thing about the world we live in today. Safe spaces can no longer be bound and limited to physical locations. Rather, they must be found and created in each of us, allowing us to transcend the limitations of walls, rooms, or a single environment. We do this by actively representing acceptance, kindness, and compassion, requiring the same in return, and displaying the courage to speak up against the inhumanity and injustices toward LGBTQIA+ people in every space we occupy.

How do we make this happen? Leadership is about creating safe spaces or representing a safe space where none exists. This is a role that will require integrity, follow-through, and courage. Growing up, I was fortunate enough to find this guidance through mentors who not only displayed leadership abilities, but also created and transformed communities and cultures. Lessons were often passed down. I had mentors who impacted the way I saw the world and my place in it, and who echoed the importance of paying it forward for others. Within these pages, I share these leadership lessons and tools through the lens of my experiences as a proud, queer Puerto Rican man, with the hopes that it will reach you to benefit you and the communities you serve. I hope that you find enlightenment, empowerment, and tools that you can make work for you. All these tools and lessons are now yours.

It's important to understand that when we talk about safe spaces, we are referring to the spaces we represent as human beings, not only a literal place.

So many times growing up, I was taught directly and indirectly that a safe space was a physical location made up of four walls and a door that could be locked, a place that I had to travel to in order to access its safety. Many times, this was supposed to mean home, school, or a family member's house. But what do you do, and where do you go, when those places aren't safe anymore?

I want to challenge you to think about the physical space that your body and voice take up in the world.

Growing up, it was hard to find safe spaces, but I managed to find safe people. I learned that unless we feel safe to blossom into our true selves, unless we can express who we are without fear and without intimidation, we can never fulfill that which we are called and destined to do in the world. Finding my safe space allowed me to understand and accept that it was okay to be gay, feminine, Boricua (people of Puerto Rican descent), and draped in all my Brown skin. It was okay that I stuttered when I got nervous or excited. It was okay to let my guard down and be open to others, and it was okay to admire other gay men as they socialized and carry on. Witnessing how they cared for one another and looked out for one another made me proud. It allowed me to feel my community's love as something tangible and real for the first time.

But what happens when our safe spaces are violated? What happens when the people we love, especially those who represent safety, are taken from us? What happens to our spirits when we can't find safety, answers, or support, and we feel hopeless and in despair? How do we deal with what we are witnessing, and where do we start picking up the pieces?

These are the questions I grappled with after the tragic Pulse incident in the summer of 2016. It was Latino Night, at two in the morning, when a lone gunman—armed with hatred, evil intent, a SIG Sauer MCX semi-automatic rifle, and a 9mm Glock 17 semi-automatic pistol—murdered forty-nine people. He made it his goal for all 320 people in attendance to experience terror like no other.

I remember that night, freezing in disbelief and horror as I watched what was happening in Orlando on the news. My heartbeat became a drum pounding louder and louder in my head. The first thing that flashed through my mind was seeing the Columbine tragedy on TV when I was twelve years old. That had been the first time I'd ever seen what a shooting looked like. It was the first time I had ever seen such terror on the faces of innocent people. And it was the first time I had ever seen blood flowing from lifeless bodies.

Pulse, however, cut me in a different way.

Just the year before, I had attended the Pulse nightclub myself. Like those at Pulse during the fateful incident, I was dancing away on a darkened and packed dance floor to the high beats of reggae with my best friend, Luis, whom we lovingly called Speedy. The strobe lights offered only quick glimpses of recognition and bathed the faces of the community all around me in flashes of light and color. The room was filled with energy, music, and a celebration of life. Looking back now, the only thing that separated me from the 2016 shooting victims was time and random chance.

The night I was at the club, it was the end of our adventurous two-week-long Miami and Orlando trip, and we chose this place as the climax. After all, Pulse is known all over the country as a must-visit hot spot, especially if you wanted to party with the Latinx and Black LGBTQIA+ community.

Entry was easy, like most gay clubs I've attended. No hassle, no dress code, no overbearing security guards (for the most part). No metal detectors—a pat down at most. Just an entry fee in hand and a valid ID, and you were good. After all, the point of these clubs has always been to create an accepting, all-inclusive safe space to be yourself and to party with others who may or may not look like you. Many clubgoers were seeking what we all seek—fun, acceptance, new friendships, and what most of us want at the end of the day, which is admiration and the respect of our community.

At the end of a long, fun night, Speedy and I were exhausted, high from the adrenaline of dancing all night, and so glad we'd made the trip. That night, I fell asleep replaying the sounds, colors, faces, and conversations from an experience I'd never forget.

But on June 12, 2016, the journey of life would be cut short, and the safe space taken from many of those who were enjoying a night out at Pulse.

Forty-nine people died in the shooting incident. Another fifty-eight were injured: fifty-three by gunfire, and five by other causes. Also, according to reports, "Thirty-eight were pronounced dead at the scene, and eleven at local hospitals. Of the thirty-eight victims to die at the scene, twenty died on the stage area and dance floor, nine in the nightclub's northern bathroom, four in the southern bathroom, three on the stage, one at the front lobby, and one out on a patio."[1] At least five of the victims were not killed during the shooter's initial volley of gunfire but during the hostage situation in the bathroom, which took law enforcement hours to end after the initial shooting rampage started. This was a tragedy of epic proportion.

Immediately following Pulse, LGBTQIA+ centers and establishments around the country went on full alert. LGBTQIA+ centers on ground floors were now having their windows blackened, doors were to always remain locked, buzzers were installed, and in some places, security guards were hired. Those friendly pat downs mentioned earlier at bars and clubs now turned into full-on frisks and searches. The idea that a gay club was targeted horrified many in the LGBTQIA+ community, and there was now a legitimate concern that others would be inspired to attack in the same way. I encountered many LGBTQIA+ individuals who were traumatized by the images of bodies carried out and the

1   Dennis Donovan, "3 Years Ago Today; The Pulse Nightclub Shooting," *Democratic Underground*, June 12, 2019, https://www.democraticunderground.com/100212181784.

stories of the horror endured inside. The number of LGBTQIA+ people seeking counseling increased everywhere.

I had been there just a year before. And I could not help but relive the night through the stories I heard on the news of people who experienced the attack. Since it was the end of Latino Night, I could not help but be taken back into the chaos that must have ensued in the haze of a good night, as the music pounded its last beats. The bathrooms I had used, the stage I had sat on, and the dance floor where I had laughed so hard were now part of horror stories where the bodies of brothers, sisters, daughters, and sons lay. *How is this real and why?* I questioned God.

I remember speaking to some of my straight family and friends who didn't even mention the incident. That lack of concern or recognition truly hurt. Not because I wanted sympathy, but because as an advocate I wanted solidarity, and the lack of acknowledgment of such a tragedy was disappointing.

And yet, in response to this tragic incident, many others in the local community and country responded with love and an outpouring of support. Blood banks had to turn people away because of the oversupply. Strangers offered to pay for medical or burial costs. Others offered emotional and trauma support. People all over the country gathered to offer any support or assistance they could. Organizations birthed from this incident include Orlando United, the onePULSE Foundation, and many others. Faith leaders from all over the state and country preached acceptance, tolerance, and love for those whose lives were lost, and compassion for those who were LGBTQIA+.

Memorials all over the country have been erected in remembrance of the lives lost at Pulse; other makeshift memorials include people's names who never made the news but were affected by gun violence just the same.

In the end, the LGBTQIA+ community was able to begin healing from the Pulse incident because they found a safe space in each other. Even with one of their greatest safe spaces devastated and other safe spaces triggering fear, they connected with one another. Their collective trauma bonded them further. Support groups flourished, vigils sprung up in places special to those who passed on, and celebrations of life were organized. Most importantly, the stories of those whose lives were lost were told. One by one, we began to truly understand the hearts and lives behind the faces and names.

We began to hear stories of the incredible values they shared with the world—values of love, kindness, and incredible fortitude. The community told narratives that would help heal the wounds of the community by choosing to focus on the greatness of each individual life, rather than the agony, terror, and horror of that night. And even though they lost their loved ones and a safe space, they became safe spaces themselves. They became a stabilizing force at a time when a community was beyond shaken by owning the narrative of their own stories and understanding that owning their experiences, however brutal, is the ultimate form of empowerment.

Creating safe spaces where none exists, and being a safe space wherever you go, will require you to tap into the attributes and skills of a leader. This includes being brave, passionate, and inspirational. It requires you to be confident, convicted in what you say, and able to spark that same belief in others. These are leadership skills that take time to develop, but are vital to nurture and possess. You can inspire and move others to evolve as they become more fully themselves.

The purpose of this book is to pass on knowledge of how to truly create safe spaces and be a safe space for yourself and others, no matter how hard things get. I'll share with you my experiences in the hopes you can relate and perhaps also find your own strength and story through the lessons I learned as an advocate.

Be courageous and ask yourself, "Do I represent a safe space? Do my values, words, and actions represent the safe space I wish to create or be? Do I represent equality, fairness, and bravery to speak up and defend someone whose voice has been taken from them or is being treaded on?"

When we move forward, are we intentional about what values we leave behind? Are we leaving our passions, our stories, and our attributes so that other generations of young people, mentees, or leaders can come along and be inspired? My hope is that we leave behind a path full of examples, which represents courage, love, and tenacity.

In Part I of this book, you will follow alongside my journey as a queer Latino boy who sought to see himself in the world. I was searching for love. I dared to dream. And I was on a quest to find my purpose. These stories are filled with examples that show the power of role models and mentors being safe spaces, as well as the lessons learned in creating safe spaces.

Part II is filled with leadership lessons I wish I had learned early on in my journey to assist with creating safe spaces, both for my community and myself. These include lessons about setting boundaries, setting a clear vision for yourself and your team, working with organizations and groups, and the power of staying in your lane. I offer tips and guidance on community building, self-care, and community peer-led and peer-driven engagement strategies.

As LGBTQIA+ leaders and advocates, you may find yourself being the first representation of a safe space, a space that allows every individual in your presence to be their authentic self.

In a world of social media and social networks, where distance and time are minimized by the touch of a button, let it be our mission not just to create physical safe spaces but to embody safe spaces. To share the values of human worth, acceptance, and self-esteem with anyone in our presence.

So, whether you are a young LGBTQIA+ person, a community-based organizer, a part of an ally organization, an LGBTQIA+

rights advocate, or someone who generally wants to become more involved in creating safe spaces, you are welcome here. My end goal is to help you recognize the leader within you and impart the confidence, clarity, and real-world lessons that will enable you to inspire those around you who need it most.

I hope throughout these pages, your self-worth and value will increase. I hope you see an example of how to cope with trauma, both internally and externally. I pray you feel empowered, heard, and understand that *you too* have a story worth telling.

A CALL TO ACTION

As one of many ways to promote safe spaces for the LGBTQIA+ community, let me start this book with a call to action that can affect everyone. Call on your lawmakers loudly to change the gun laws in this country. Reach out to your local representatives, engaging in community and civic engagement, or support others in the community who are leading this fight. Because it is and will continue to be a fight.

Since June 12, 2016, more than 100,000 people have been killed by gun violence in the US. Despite numerous proposals and legislative efforts by lawmakers to pass measures to stop the bloodshed, no major gun violence prevention legislation has been signed into law since 1994.[2]

Gun violence is tearing through our country. Even as I write this in mid-September 2021 and we are beginning to re-open from COVID, in the background, my CNN ticker reads: "470 Mass Shootings This Year."

Yet we will not let hate and violence win. We will continue to demand justice and create safe spaces all over the world. And

2   HRC Staff, "Three Years Since Pulse, Lawmakers Must Act to Address Ongoing Epidemic of Gun Violence," *Human Rights Campaign*, June 11, 2019, https://www.hrc.org/news/three-years-since-pulse -lawmakers-must-act-to-address-ongoing-epidemic-of-g.

today, Pulse stands as a symbol of hope. Never forget that in the midst of all that is bad in the world, good can still be born from it.

This story…my story…and your story—are stories of hope and triumph.

Part 1

My Journey from a Bullied Brown Boy to a Proud Latino Gay Man and Community Leader

"Never be bullied into silence. Never allow yourself to be made a victim. Accept no one's definition of your life; define yourself."

—HARVEY FIERSTEIN

CHAPTER 1

Growing Up Different

"I believe that telling our stories, first to ourselves and then to
one another and the world, is a revolutionary act."

—JANET MOCK, AUTHOR, TV HOST, AND TRANSGENDER RIGHTS ACTIVIST

Even the calmness of the blue sky would not stop me from running
until I was safe. This was life now in the Stella Wright Projects
on Prince and Spruce Street, on the south side of Newark. Being
Latino, slightly feminine, a stutterer, and born with a port-wine
stain birthmark over my left eye made me unmistakably noticed
and remembered. Each afternoon as I navigated home from Quit-
man Street School, I knew I could be bullied at any moment, as I
had so often experienced. Navigating through a maze of endless
brown and ashy brick buildings and blackened dirty asphalt only
added to my anxiety of the unknown, but it also awakened my
curiosity of what seemed like a new planet to me.

Just a year earlier, at nine years old, I had lived in a different
neighborhood in Newark made up of Puerto Ricans, Dominicans,
Cubans, and South Americans. There was a bodega on every
corner, and no family houses were more than three stories high
in the Central Ward.

There, I had belonged. Each home was sure to have a makeshift garden of some kind, a Puerto Rican flag hanging from the window or car. And if your grandparents were straight from the islands, like mine were, live chickens or roosters were likely not far away.

I was my family's designated errand boy, which mainly meant running to the bodegas for my grandmother Virginia and my aunt's vital dinner items, such as Goya rice, sofrito, or sazón, and their not-so-vital items like Newport 100s, scratch offs, and lottery tickets. I always excitedly volunteered, with the intent of pocketing the change to get penny candy after a long day of store runs.

At the end of the week, like clockwork, the elderly men of the block played dominos on homemade tables, sitting on metal foldable chairs or milk crates, puffing on their cigars. Meanwhile, salsa, bachata, and merengue music danced ever so faintly through the air, a sound that often collided with the most delicious smells I have ever known. It all signaled the weekend was here, that my aunts, uncles, and cousins were coming over, and that my grandmother was bringing her magical dishes to life in the kitchen. She made arroz con gandules, with an incredibly delectable sofrito producing an aroma that would permeate all of the apartments in the house. She also made bacalaítos, or greasy little salted codfish fritters, and pernil—a succulent pork roast. Life was easy back then.

My mother, twin brother Angel, and I shared a three-story house with our family. My great-grandma lived on the first floor; we lived on the second floor with my grandma, aunt Wanda, and two uncles, Louie and Franky; and my great-aunt Carmen lived on the third floor with my cousins. We had a full house, and needless to say, there was always another family member coming over for dinner or popping up out of the blue. As my aunt and uncles got older and started going to high school, it became apparent to my mom we needed to move and create a home of our own.

As soon as public housing was offered to us, Mom jumped at

the opportunity to provide for my brother and me. For the first time, we would have our own beds and bedrooms.

And so, at ten years old, I found myself moving into the seventh floor of a twelve-story building in the middle of the projects. A few weeks prior, my mom sat my brother and me down and explained that our new apartment was ready and assigned through a city lottery system. When I heard lottery, all I pictured was the old white publishing house man that rang your doorbell and handed you a gigantic check with a handful of balloons. Little did I know this "lottery" was for low-income families who needed public housing assistance. Our small family unit hadn't changed, but everything else was about to.

MY MOM: FROM YOUNG LOVE TO SINGLE PARENTHOOD

My mom is from the Bronx and my dad is from Newark. Both second-generation Puerto Ricans. Both young teens—Mom was thirteen and my dad was fifteen—when they met and had a typical teenage love affair, during which my mom got pregnant. Both were, of course, living with their parents, navigating life with what skills they had. Unfortunately, by the time my mom was ready to deliver us, my dad had slowly exited the scene. He got involved in drugs and partying. Overnight, she became a single fourteen-year-old Latina mom with two twin boys and no trade or education to rely on.

We were homeless quite a bit during my early childhood. As a smart five-year-old, walking around aimlessly with my mom and my brother, I had an understanding that we didn't always have a place to go. One day, standing outside a Burger King, I overheard a phone call my mom made to my dad's parents—my grandmother Lucy and my grandfather Juan—telling them they needed to come get us because she just couldn't do it right now. We had no place to go, and she needed some time to get things together. In a heartbeat, my grandmother and grandfather came through to pick us up, and my brother and I stayed with them for a couple of years until Mom pulled herself together enough to come back for us.

My dad's mom was an artist by trade, and the go-to lady for the centerpieces and giveaways at family parties and baby showers. She cooked for everyone in the neighborhood and often catered events. My dad's dad was a larger-than-life man at 6'5". He was kind, smart, loving, and an exceptional provider for his family. I remember how hard he worked as an importer and exporter for Latinx supermarkets, and the long hours that came with that. Still, he would come home after a long day of work, pick us up, throw us into the air to catch us, and lift our shirts and blow raspberries on our stomachs with his beard tickling us. He made us feel so loved each time he walked in the door. He was a giant in our eyes.

Angel and I lived with my dad's parents from the age of five until eight. During this time, Mom became more settled and came back for us. We then moved with my mom's mom, Virginia, into the three-family house I mentioned earlier.

During this time, Mom took up a bartending gig at a bar in our neighborhood as a means to support us. Her customers adored her. The days Angel and I would be there with her, they would always buy us a bag of chips, sodas, and a Slim-Jim. On very lucky days, mostly Fridays, a few would give us a dollar.

My mom let us sit with her on the high stools at the bar before it opened for the evening, serving us a Coke in a fancy glass, refilling the bowl of peanuts as we waited for our dinner to be delivered or our babysitter to pick us up for the night. I used to study my mom's face as she stocked the bar and tended to her early customers, and I watched their faces, too. They seemed to glow with excitement when she spoke to them, which wasn't a surprise as to me, she always glowed. My mother is beautiful and charming, with a lot of Bronx sass. Think Rosario Dawson's elegance sprinkled with the spunk, attitude, and loudness of Rosie Perez.

But at the age of ten, our lives changed as we began a new chapter in the Stella Wright Projects, and I adjusted to a world I had never known existed. The good news was that we were not homeless that time around. The bad news was our new home was in the toughest projects in the city. The buildings at Stella Wright looked like skyscrapers to me. But instead of feeling a sense of awe, I felt tiny and insignificant. Even on a warm spring day, the shadows created by the encircling buildings would block out the sun, a reminder of how dark and cold life could become there.

MY FIRST EXPERIENCE WITH HIV/AIDS

In the spring of 1993, as I was walking home through the project complex, I came to the edge of a small, dusty dirt and clay field where all the neighborhood kids played.

I stopped and scanned the wide-open field we had made into our playground and noticed a woman sitting in the gold-colored dirt, wearing what looked like a light blue and white hospital gown. As I approached her, what struck me most wasn't the strangeness of her being almost naked, hot, and lethargic while sitting on the bare, unforgiving ground. It was that this woman had physical features I recognized in my mom and aunts. She was Latina, and up to this point, I had never seen any other Latin person there who was not related to me.

She wasn't wearing shoes and didn't appear to be wearing much else but the gown. No more than eighty pounds, she was only a skeleton frame of a woman. Her arms and legs were covered in open sores, and her busy fingers picked invisible scabs off her legs. Her sunken eyes were dazed and blackened, staring into an abyss of space and a time long ago, perhaps one that wasn't so dark, desperate, and hot. The sun blazed relentlessly on her, a cool occasional breeze her fleeting savior.

By the fourth grade, I knew what a drug addict looked like. Still, a sense of urgency flooded me as I rushed upstairs and burst into the kitchen to tell my mother there was a Spanish lady sitting in the dirt next to our building in a blue hospital gown. Immediately, a look of concern and acknowledgment flashed across my mom's eyes, and she hurried downstairs. I followed as fast as I could down the many flights of stairs, past the drug dealers standing in the lobby. The neighborhood kids scattered when we reached the field. Shockingly, my mom recognized this shell of a woman, calling her Naomi within seconds.

"Naomi? Who's Naomi?" I mumbled under my breath.

Visibly shaken, she gently scooped up Naomi into her arms, not concerned about any of the sores on her delicate frame, and carried her back through the field and project complex, back to our home. I could see the determination in my mother's eyes as she carried her through the complex, staring ahead as if on a solo mission. Around us, people were chatting, staring, and pointing. *Why isn't anyone offering my mom help?* I thought as I worked to stay near her hip to provide any support that I could.

Imagine rows and rows of twelve-story buildings housing thousands of people, but not maintaining basic human services for those tenants. Everyone threw away their trash daily or weekly, but there was nowhere for it to go. Without consistent trash collection, people threw bags of trash and loose items into the stairwells, out the windows, into every open space they could. The stairwells constantly smelled like urine and rotting food, and the filth made the stairs sticky and slippery at times. Added to the dim lighting in the stairwells that would flicker on and off unpredictably, and stay off predictably, it wasn't uncommon to walk in complete and treacherous darkness to make it to the next flight. It was the only way to get to our apartment, a daunting journey on our passage to safety.

Undeterred, Mom carried Naomi in her arms through the

trash and darkness, up seven flights of stairs, and laid her on our couch. That was the first time I recognized my mom as both being incredibly strong and extremely delicate at the same time, but it wouldn't be the last.

My mom took care of Naomi day in and day out, feeding her, bathing her, and changing her, as we learned more about her condition. In the coming days, my mother uncomfortably explained that Naomi was our aunt. I was confused as to why I never had heard of this aunt before. She went on to tell us that she had moved away with a boyfriend, leaving her daughter with my great-grandma. She continued to explain that my aunt unfortunately got sick from injecting drugs and was diagnosed with AIDS.

"AIDS? What is AIDS?" I asked.

My mother swiftly replied, dropping her big brown eyes to avoid looking at me. "AIDS is what happens when you don't take care of yourself. Or you're not careful who you hang out with."

Her response didn't make sense to me, but I had a feeling that I should not, or could not, explore that answer any further. Especially after my mother's follow-up directive: "You're a child, Julio, so stay in a child's place." This was her go-to response when I asked "Why?" one too many times, or butted into grown folks' business or conversations.

Because of her shame, by the time Naomi got visibly sick, she had severed her connections to our family and moved away from us all. This was why I hadn't known of her before that day in the field. Now, as she laid on our couch, and after a few doctors' visits foretelling of her fate, our family warned my mom: "She shouldn't be in your house, Rosa. She's going to get you guys sick, Rosa," and "Be careful with your boys." But Mom wouldn't hear any of it. She gave Naomi her own set of utensils, her own plate, and anything else to reduce contact, and she bleached everything nonstop.

During those first few days, Mom educated my brother and me about HIV and AIDS, explaining as best she could how you could get it, and how you cannot. She told us "not to judge some-one or treat them badly just because they're sick," that everyone needs the love of someone else, and that those with HIV or who are sick simply need more love.

I could tell mom was afraid for my aunt's life at times, often sitting with Naomi's head in her lap as she gently rubbed it. She did everything she could to let my aunt know that she was loved and worthy, regardless of the path she'd taken in life.

My mom showed me pictures of Naomi when she was younger, sharing stories about how she was always so proud of her long, black, beautifully thick hair, and how they would always sneak away, being the two oldest kids. Now I watched as my mom combed Naomi's few remaining hairs as if they were little girls all over again.

Naomi could not communicate. She could look at us, turn her head toward us, and occasionally sigh. Some days I sat on the couch just watching her, as her breathing would get heavier, not understanding the full reality of what was happening.

I remember looking into her eyes and wondering what she was experiencing, and what she might want to say if she could. Her steady stares with her hollow, darkened eyes scared me, her desperate look of longing forever etched in my memory.

Three weeks into her stay with us, her breathing became labored, and I could hear the intense rattle of her body barely clinging to life. At two in the morning one day, I was abruptly awakened by my mom screeching and moaning—a haunting, primal sound like no other.

My brother and I ran into the living room and saw our uncle Tony crying, supporting himself against the wall. Naomi had just exhaled her last breath.

Mom was now rocking our aunt's frail body, holding her, mourning in a way that scared me. I have never seen my mom—my protector, my everything—this way, grieving as only a caregiver can. Seeing that kind of heartache and pain frightened me.

Still a caretaker, my mom rubbed lavender oil over Naomi's forehead and lips to keep her skin moisturized. Then she combed her hair one last time, almost in a ritualistic way, as if to honor their bond and say goodbye.

The funeral caretaker showed up alone, with no one to help him, so my uncle helped. The few relatives who were in our home took my mom away. Then my uncle and the coroner carried Naomi's body down the same stairs she'd traveled up three weeks earlier while in my mother's arms.

We'll never know how she made the trek to our apartment wearing nothing but a hospital gown. Perhaps it was divine guidance leading her to us in the hopes that she'd be recognized—that even in her lowest moments, she'd find a safe space to be seen, accepted, and loved.

Although Naomi's departure was incredibly sad, her arrival, and my mother's response to her, planted a seed in me that foretold a story of hope, courage, and determination. It would eventually lead to the need to search for and the creation of safe spaces for anyone who may find themselves in need of safety.

Watching my mother's courage and ability to care for my aunt, regardless of what anyone else was saying, left me in awe. This woman whom I had come to know as my ultimate caretaker and everything in life was able to share that same love and compassion to someone whom others would not touch or go near. I felt my mother's fear, but I could only see the courage.

ALWAYS ON GUARD

I learned to adapt to my new surroundings. I had to quickly become more assertive and stand up for myself, which was a frightening prospect for such an awkward, quiet kid. I hardly spoke to anyone; I didn't know how to, and also, I was scared.

My meek demeanor and shy presence led the neighborhood kids to pick on me, so my goal was to avoid the groups of boys on the playground, but hopefully make a friend in the process. I learned quick that in the projects, you are either testing someone or getting tested to see who you are and where you stand in defending yourself. So I fought back when forced to and learned to defend myself as best I could whether I lost or won.[3]

The projects were flooded with violence. Our block on Spruce Street was known as the place to buy weapons as well as drugs. Every entrance to my building, from the lobby to the stairwell, had a pocket of drug dealers selling in every direction. I literally never knew what was around the next corner. And so, between the ages of ten and thirteen, when most kids and their parents should be focused on thriving, my family's concern was surviving, navigating, and always thinking ahead. This was the reality of the many families in the projects.

I was fortunate that my family name was known in the streets, as some of my relatives were respected drug and weapons dealers. Many Spruce Street dealers stepped in to intervene when they saw me in trouble, getting picked on, or circled, because of the high esteem they held for my uncles.

My teenage male cousins saw what I went through growing up, always getting bullied, so they were protective of me. They hung out on the playground outside my school and made it known that they weren't quiet and meek like I was. I remember being so embarrassed by their loudness. Sometimes their protection and presence worked for me, and sometimes it didn't. I was just grateful for the times it did, because it kept me from having to physically defend myself on that day.

3   Please see Appendix C at the end of the book for Helpful LGBTQIA+ Resources.

THE FIRST AWARENESS OF BEING DIFFERENT

I first became aware that I was different around eleven years old when I realized I liked boys. This feeling didn't seem foreign to me, but somehow, as I sensed the urge increasing, I knew I could not express that excitement for another boy in any way. Soon after, I discovered *Bop* magazine at Kmart and became even more confused, and the start of my curiosity began. *Bop* was a series of fan magazines that had pictures and interviews of all of the famous teenage male actors, such as Devon Sawa, Brad Renfro, Johnathan Taylor Thomas, and Macaulay Culkin. Even at that age, I remember looking for other Black and Brown boys to no success.

My favorites were Macaulay Culkin and Johnathan Taylor Thomas, one of the sons on *Home Improvement.* I knew it wasn't the same way I liked my school "girlfriends" at the time. I fantasized about simple things like going to the park together, or holding hands, or kissing. As if I knew anything about kissing at eleven years old. But then, I immediately shut down those kinds of thoughts because it didn't seem normal to me; I didn't see any of my male friends walking around holding hands with other boys. I realized without being told it was probably something I shouldn't be doing, especially in the hood where I lived. I knew almost instinctively I could never own the magazine, as it would make me stand out as different, something that would put another target on my back, and I did not want that.

I hid behind my shy behavior so I wouldn't do anything that would draw attention to myself. I thought, *I'm just gonna look at these magazines when it's safe and keep my true feelings to myself.* This only happened when I visited Kmart and could break away from my family for a few moments. All I knew was those magazines—and my daydreams—had to stay at Kmart and far away from my real life.

If the kids at school had known I was daydreaming about boys like the girls in class did, they would've called me "fag" or "faggot" really quick. Kids at my school used that word a lot when addressing the more feminine or "proper-acting" boys. I was quiet and had the tendency to be more open or loose only if I got too comfortable with someone, so I never let myself get too comfortable with anyone. I learned to be invisible, to pass as one of them, by burying my voice, laughing, and doing what kids do to try to fit in.

When I observed bullying or name-calling at school or in the projects, I kept my comments to myself. I was not confrontational and would occasionally laugh to deflect the things the feminine boys would do or say to react. Their fearlessness intrigued me, but their authenticity terrified me. Sometimes, it felt as though they knew I was one of them, a part of the "family," which was further confirmed by the "mm-hmm" stares I would get from them, accompanied by a roll of the eyes and a tilt of their head.

By twelve, I *knew* I was different. Watching my uncles' and cousins' male friends come over to hang out and play basketball further confirmed that. I didn't know I was gay, per se, and I can't say it was sexual either. But I definitely was drawn to them and attracted to them.

SILENT SUPPORT, SEXUAL ABUSE, AND AN UNLIKELY MENTOR

Looking back, my grandmother, Virginia, noticed that I was different and likely sensed I was gay. She tried her best to make me feel good about myself no matter what, always providing a safe space for me in her home. I think about her a lot because of the acceptance she so lovingly provided at a time in my life when I didn't even know I needed or wanted it. Her home, her time, and her presence became a refuge for me.

Always working, my grandmother sold Avon cosmetics as a side job, and she would give me the catalog to look at when she babysat me on weekends. I loved to flip through the pages of the small book, look at all the colorful products and happy models, and race to scratch off all the cologne and perfumes tabs first. When a new issue came out, she handed that catalog to me and let me pick one item out, like lip balm, body mist, or scented lotion. She gently steered me away from the more blatantly feminine items, perhaps to protect me from the bullying that would surely ensue if anyone saw me using them. But if I insisted, she bought it for me anyway and kept it at her house.

On our many car rides, out of the blue, she would say things like, "I don't care if I ever have a grandchild who is different. I'm always going to accept them and love them." At twelve years old, I didn't really know what she was talking about, or why she said things like this so often, but I filed her words away in my head. My grandmother was my first mentor and advocate.

My schoolteachers were another source of acceptance and refuge. I had several amazing teachers who often pulled me aside to check on me and encouraged me to sign up for extracurricular activities. They often allowed me to eat my lunch in the classrooms, away from the other students, when they sensed I needed a break from the bullying.

Little did I know my school had a mentoring program in which ten students were chosen and assigned a mentor from outside the community. My teachers selected me to participate. When I first learned I was getting a mentor, I was elated; they explained I was one of only ten participants and that I had many great experiences to look forward to. And so, at the age of twelve, I was matched with my first mentor, Stanley Fisher.

Stanley was the Director of Consumer Affairs for New Jersey and worked in downtown Newark. He was white, in his fifties, and lived in South Jersey. The mentor's goal was to be a role model, provide guidance, and allow the mentee to have experiences outside the community they lived in. He committed to weekly outings and would drive into the projects to pick me up.

The experiences were many. We would go to the comic book store, to the library, mini golfing, bowling, to the movies, or to his house in the South Shore to spend time with his family.

At first, even though I was excited, I was suspicious and incredibly guarded. At this point in my life, I had already experienced sexual abuse by someone close to the family. So, each time I got in Stanley's car, I thought he had the same intentions and motivations for being nice to me. I just knew what would happen sooner or later: he'd touch me in the wrong way, or he'd ask me to do something I didn't want to do. But he never touched me or had an inappropriate conversation with me. I was relieved. I was glad. But I was also terribly confused. I thought to myself, *Why does he do this? What's in it for him?* Thankfully, after a few months of spending time with him, I finally learned to relax around him and his family. And that's when I started learning about the wider world of possibilities.

My regular outings with my mentor gave me my first taste of life outside the inner city. I had also never spent much time around white people or white families. As a Brown Latino kid, there were many things I made up in my mind about how white people lived. I quickly found out that most of the preconceptions I had about white people from watching TV really didn't check out.

He treated me like a son, creating a safe space for me as an additional family member. The mentoring experience was the most fascinating and adventurous thing I'd experienced in my life to that point. But I felt guilty that my twin brother, Angel, was not having these amazing experiences with me.

DARING TO DREAM

As the Director of Consumer Affairs, Stanley was very influential, a leader I had the opportunity to watch up close. Leaving the inner city on a regular basis opened my eyes to how other people lived, how other communities functioned, and the fact that I didn't have to stay in the projects if I didn't want to. *I had a choice.*

These experiences and having a mentor fed my imagination, gave me a broader worldview, and helped me cope with my everyday environment. Every time I was introduced to something or someone new, I added it to my internal file folder of who I wanted to become and what I wanted to do with my own life. I remember thinking, *There's a whole world out there, and I want to be a part of it!* The trips with Stanley had an amazing impact on my ability to dream.

A year into my mentorship, I had the opportunity to job shadow Stanley by visiting his office once a week and interacting with his team, which taught me that with a little curiosity, you can learn from anyone.

Although the mentoring commitment through the school program was only for a year, Stanley continued to mentor me for several years. He taught me my imagination was the key to my future, and that my only limitations were those I set upon myself. He expanded my world and showed me there is more to life than wondering if you'll make it up the seven dark and dangerous floors home. Outside of my family, he was the first person who really cared about me.

There was a downside to my good fortune, though. While I was out experiencing a completely different way of life, my twin brother was left at home, waiting for me to return with exciting stories and memorabilia.

Angel and I had always been treated differently. My brother was more my protector than I was for him, even though I was technically older by three minutes. He was always way bigger than me, had tons of energy, was super curious and a dreamer, and wanted to meet new people. Sadly, these qualities made him easy prey to the local street drug dealers and shady characters. I can still remember cringing when people would say, "Julio is the good one, and Angel is the bad one." I'm sure this did nothing to build up his self-worth.

THE GIFT OF A GREAT IMAGINATION

Boy, did I have an imagination as a kid. When my mom used to head out for work at 11:30 every night, leaving me and my brother home alone, her absence created anxiety and fear in me. I'd worry, thinking, *My mom's about to leave. What will happen?* I'd imagine ten different scenarios and try to think through all of them so I'd be prepared. *What do I do if someone we don't know knocks on the door? What if my brother gets in trouble? What if someone tries to break in?*

Movies like *Home Alone* did *not* help my anxiety, even though it was my favorite movie. And I've already told you how I felt about Macaulay Culkin.

I used my imagination to create a place where I was the leader and I was in charge. My brother and I sometimes made cookies at two in the morning where I was the head baker. We created game nights on our Nintendo, playing all night, or prank calling people from the phone book.

As harsh as the projects were, I had many great firsts there, like my first kiss with a boy as I played hide-and-seek with my brother's friends. Or my first schoolyard love matches, brought on by the admiration of the girls who would slip me notes, asking, "Do you want to be my boyfriend? Yes or no." I also met my first two girl best friends, Ameerah and Sarah, who often protected me from those boys who always called me Rico Suave and decided I should fight to keep that name. A name I didn't want.

While I dealt with the stressors of life by projecting a future that seemed much more hopeful than my bleak situation, my twin brother had a different coping mechanism. He was always into mischief and trouble, and the circumstances were getting worse.

Due to increasing gang violence and targeted bullying, when I was thirteen, we had to move out of the projects and into Newark's North Ward, called Little Puerto Rico.

A DEPARTURE FROM THE PROJECTS
AND A NEW DAD

Aunt Dolly, my biological father's sister, also lived in North Newark and was a fantastic force in my upbringing. She hired me to babysit my four younger cousins when I was thirteen, my first paying gig, so she could go to dinner or the lounge with her husband and our other family members. I lived for these weekends, secretly listening to Madonna with my cousins, having fashion shows with them, and producing them in fantasy plays and skits.

Since my cousins were still young, I was able to be the real me, the me I was when the grown-ups weren't around, and my cousins didn't judge me for that. Johnathan, Mark, and Jay were all under the age of ten, and my one girl cousin, Crystal, was eight and the star of every show. Crystal is still my best friend to this day.

That time with them allowed me to exist truthfully in a wildly creative space without judgment. They were always innocently excited to have their favorite older cousin over every weekend, putting on all these pretend productions of Britney Spears and No Doubt concerts.

I knew my aunt knew I was different, even though she never said a word about it. She simply offered a safe space where I could be myself, no questions asked. It was a liberating feeling before I even knew the totality of safe spaces.

By then, my mother had finally met someone special who would become my stepfather, the man I call Dad. David Taylor was a twenty-eight-year-old Black man from North Carolina with a heavy southern accent. He had a huge sense of humor and an even bigger heart. His example of selflessness in raising me and my brother at one of the most important times in our lives was priceless. Both he and my grandfather showed me what it meant to be a provider and hard worker. But his patience was definitely tested as my brother continued to get into trouble.

I'm sure the lead poisoning didn't help his behavioral impulses, nor mine.

THE LONG-TERM EFFECTS OF LEAD POISONING

Over a decade earlier, my mother had lived in housing that offered daycare services for teen moms, so my three-year-old brother and I stayed in the daycare while she worked. Free childcare was a definite perk. But the downside was that without much direct supervision, and being two very curious boys, we had discovered a way to entertain ourselves—peeling lead-infused paint chips off the walls and eating them. Over the course of several months, and unbeknownst to my mom, we, along with several other kids, ate *a lot* of paint chips and ended up getting lead poisoning from the daycare. It was so bad we almost died.

The first signs that something was wrong were the constant seizures me and my brother would have during the early morning hours. In fact, after two weeks in the hospital and many tests, the doctors told my mother that due to our severe exposure, we would both suffer from retardation, a term I would never use but at the time was pretty common. Mom was told that we would not be able to read or write, and that we would have extreme developmental issues with our motor skills, like stuttering and poor balance and coordination.

We both stayed in the hospital for months so the nurses could give us shots in our legs three times a day. The shot included an agent that would bind to metal so that the toxins could be eliminated in our kidneys. My brother and I had scabs from the tops of our thighs all the way down to our ankles. Even after we went home, my mom was up with us several times a night for a few years because we both experienced seizures from the lead poisoning until it completely filtered out of our bodies.

The severity of the lead poisoning definitely affected my brother and I differently. While I didn't experience learning difficulties or issues with delayed reading or motor skills, my brother started to act out unpredictably. Doctors didn't realize back then that children who have been exposed to extreme levels of lead poisoning are at an increased risk for behavioral difficulties.

At the age of thirteen, my brother began breaking into houses and cars, stealing, selling drugs, and getting involved with the local gang. At school, he got into physical altercations with students and teachers, even the principal. It was almost as if he had become a magnet for trouble, and *only* trouble. As a result of these fights, my mom or my stepdad would have to leave work to pick him up from the principal's office or the police station. After a while, my brother's constant bad behavior ultimately cost my stepdad his job. He was fired for missing too many days or having to leave early.

My parents couldn't afford to leave work anymore, so they didn't resist when my brother wanted to drop out of school. Unfortunately, half of my family had dropped out of school to find work, take care of a new baby, or support the family in another way—whatever reason made sense at the time.

Left to right: my twin brother, Angel, and me (1987)

Stella Wright housing projects, seen from 18th Ave and Prince St.,
Newark, NJ (1998). Credit: Camilo José Vergara

My mom, Rosario Perez (1989)

Left to right: my twin brother, Angel, my grandmother,
Virginia, and me (1991)

CHAPTER 2

Higher Calling

"Widen the path of opportunities and continue to leave
a powerful and positive legacy in this world."

—LUIS FONSI, SINGER AND SONGWRITER

While my brother, Angel, spent more of his life on the streets, I
grew in the opposite direction. After we left the Stella Wright
projects, we moved to North Newark, where I finally made two
new best friends, Emma and Latoya. They made going to school
feel safer, especially when bullying went from verbal attacks in
the projects to more physical attacks at Rafael Hernandez Ele-
mentary School.

When we first moved to North Newark, I was excited. I
believed that moving into a Latinx community with other kids
who looked like me would lessen the teasing and name-calling.
But the bullying got worse. I quickly realized that I didn't look
like the other light-skinned, blue-, green-, or gray-eyed Puerto
Ricans who all hung out with one another, and my family didn't
have a lot of connections in the community. I also didn't have
the latest gadgets like the other kids did, and my mom could not
afford the North Face or Timberland boots that made everyone
so cool. I hated gym class, didn't play a team sport, and refused

to chase any girls around. As a darker-skinned Puerto Rican with an afro, I didn't fit in with them, and eventually, the name-calling was accompanied by kicks, punches, and more face-to-face confrontations.

I was perplexed; in the projects, I sometimes felt I was not a part of the community because I was not Black and I didn't look like anyone else there. But now, in a Latinx community, I was being treated worse. *What's wrong with me? What's it about me that they don't like? What will they use about me to humiliate me tomorrow?* I pushed these questions aside every day after school as I walked up the hill so I could leave the day behind me. But they only greeted me every morning when I woke up. Having Emma and Latoya as my refuge kept me from dropping out of school or worst.

At home, I always tried to be a well-behaved son to take some of the stress off Mom because of how much she worried about Angel and making ends meet. When I would hear about my brother getting into trouble or hanging with the wrong crowd, I didn't always tell my mom, both to shield her and to protect my brother. Being honest to Mom was always important, but being loyal to my twin brother so he would not get in trouble always seemed to trump that need for honesty. Especially if I knew he would have to deal with discipline from my stepdad.

Up to this point, I had not really thought much about God except for the stories my stepdad would share, stories told to him by his parents and grandparents.

One summer Sunday morning, on my walk back home from spending the weekend at my grandma Virginia's house, I took a different route to prolong and enjoy the walk. Soon, I found myself walking toward a huge yellow building I had passed many times before. It filled nearly a whole city block. As I got closer, I could hear the most amazing music through the front doors. There were tambourines and drums, people singing and shouting. The joyful but strange sound made me curious, so I slowed down, looked through the darkly tinted glass doors, and watched beautifully clothed people two-stepping back and forth.

I cracked open the heavy wood-and-gold-framed door and stuck my head inside. Instantly, vibrations of sound reverberated through me as the whole congregation praised and worshipped God. A beautiful Black woman with the most amazing smile waved to invite me in. This woman had a glow I had never seen, and her eyes were so full of light, compassion, and love. I instantly felt safe.

Intrigued, I stepped inside and slid into one of the red velvety seats at the back of the sanctuary to watch. The music had awakened something in me. Who were these people? They were dancing and crying and praying aloud and speaking in languages I'd never heard before.

After service was over that day, I knew I would return. Little did I know my stepdad's best friend, Ray, was encouraging him and my mom to visit this same congregation.

On my third visit, and after prompting from my stepdad, my mother and brother finally attended. The pastor made the same announcement he'd made at the end of the two Sunday services I'd attended before. He offered a relationship with Jesus Christ and the ability to be saved. Through Christ, he told us we could have a place with God forever, a place where there is no pain or suffering and you are forever engulfed in God's pure and everlasting love for all eternity. It was also a way to avoid Hell and separation from God and His love forever.

The thought of *that* scared me to death, so my choice seemed easy. My brother and I nervously followed my mother to the front of the church during the altar call. We were all getting saved. All the pastors, deacons, and congregants intently stared at us as we approached the altar. The stoic senior pastor, cloaked in a purple velvet and gold robe, smiled broadly at us, breaking the serious façade that, up to this point, had intimidated me.

"Welcome, daughter," he said as he laid hands on my mom. "Welcome, son," he followed, placing oil on each of our foreheads. He said a prayer over us that started in English and then went into an unknown language I later learned was called "speaking in tongues."

My mom began to cry, and I remember being a little confused but understanding something life changing was happening to us. We then repeated the Sinner's Prayer. As we did this, every member of the church got up and started praying out loud and lifting their hands toward us. Some were praying in tongues, some were praising God, and some had tears in their eyes while they watched us. Others were rebuking the Devil, shouting, "You will not have this family! This family will be free!"

I was saved that day, and I could feel it; an overwhelming feeling of peace and stillness was tangible to me like never before. There was something bigger than me, and I knew it. This church became my new safe space.

Mom saw how excited I was to find a place where I felt like I belonged. She began budgeting bus fare for me to attend because she knew it was a way to keep me out of trouble and occupied. It was an hour-and-a-half ride and required two buses: the #27 New Jersey transit bus to downtown Newark, and then bus #24 on Broad and Market up Central Avenue. I still have vivid memories of riding the city bus to church alone, with my Bible under my arm, getting stares but not caring one bit about what anyone thought. I was a child of God now, after all. I finally belonged somewhere.

I wanted to learn everything and began reading every book in my path. I sought the wisdom and time of the leadership team. I was all about community involvement with my church. I wanted to be out in the streets with the microphone, getting people saved. I wanted to be anywhere in public where we could spread the Gospel. I wanted to bring attention to the message of salvation and a loving relationship with God. I wanted people to experience what I had experienced: salvation, peace, safety, unconditional love, and most of all, an outlet to discover my calling and natural leadership abilities.

A GOD-GIVEN PLATFORM

Church gave me my first leadership platform. The ministry got to know me and saw my natural skills, so they helped me believe in myself. They instilled in me that I was gifted and meant to do great things with my life. They provided me opportunities to grow by providing me opportunities to try. They even allowed me to lead prayers, and several years later, I was leading and teaching Saturday youth classes. Soon, I was leading city-wide youth prayer efforts, laying hands, and was fully engaged in ministry. I traveled to conferences, teaching and learning from others the latest movements in the youth church, and discovering the incredible power that comes with being both a servant of God and a leader. They helped me understand that I was a leader in my own right, and I realized that I had to conduct myself in a way that was respectable of that title.

By this time, I was attending every evening meeting, prayer group, and Sunday service by myself, even if no one else in my family would come with me.

The senior pastor and his staff were my mentors and role models. They carried themselves in such a way that people were instantly magnetized to them, no matter where they were. I remember thinking, *When I get older, that's the kind of presence I want to exude when I walk into a room.* Obviously, they were not all perfect. But they instilled in me very early on that I was destined to lead, and that God had specifically chosen me for something special that nobody else could do. This fed my imagination, and I was able to see how boundless my life could truly become. They filled me with their empowering words and thoughts until they became my thoughts and words, too, and I knew to my core that I had something special to give the world.

However, by the time I turned fifteen, I experienced a conflict, at least internally, that came with conducting myself in a way that was "respectable" of being a leader in a prominent Black church. *I was gay.* I wasn't out yet to anyone, but I knew it. I could feel this conflict within myself, brewing and bubbling up inside of me, struggling to stay quiet. Yet I wanted to shout my truth from the rooftops. I prayed about it. I cried about it. I questioned God, begging Him to explain how it was even possible that He could use me to lay hands, preach, or teach. If I was sinning and an abomination, how could the church use me? It made me question at times whether I was hearing from God, or if He could even hear me.

To be clear, I do believe that you can be gay *and* have a relationship with God. I wholeheartedly believe that the God of your understanding loves you and there is nothing sinful with being gay whatsoever. But back then, I felt torn because these people at church absolutely loved me, but I knew they didn't know the *real* me. They didn't know how sad I was that I couldn't share my truth, how I always felt like I was looking in from the outside, and how I doubted that they'd still accept me if they knew my secret.

THE INTERNAL STRUGGLE

To hide the stress of struggling within, I played another role yet again. I was being mentored to become a leader of one of the biggest churches in Newark, so naturally I started dating a ministry leader's daughter. When I say "naturally," I mean that we had been friends for a few years, and she was the most beautiful girl I had ever seen. All of our interactions occurred at church. We sat together during services and taught youth classes together on Saturdays, and we followed each other around in between.

Her smile, presence, and the way she carried herself made me so nervous and giddy.

As much as we tried to play the roles and enjoyed each other's company, that spark was never big enough to have an actual boyfriend-and-girlfriend relationship. We didn't talk about our personal preferences out loud, but we were quite comfortable with each other as friends. Any attempts at more and it would just become uncomfortable, like a puzzle piece that just didn't fit. What we had was a genuine friendship, but there was no chemistry.

I believe we both *knew* I was different.

I took her to prom and did all of the things that were expected of a male courting a female, but our interactions were awkward and forced when we played those roles. I stayed in perpetual conflict with my sexuality because of my place in the church, and also coming from a Latinx family in which no one had ever come out or identified as gay or lesbian. I thought I was condemned to go to Hell. I always ended up going home and crying in my solitude because I believed my attraction to men, and the love I dreamed of having with another man, was an abomination.

I wanted to serve God for most of my adolescent life, but I was convinced that I had to hide who I really was in order to become His servant. So, I just kept pushing and praying the gay away, and pulling "my girlfriend" toward me to solidify and conform to society's heterosexual norms.

At fifteen, I already understood power dynamics very well. I'd heard pastors preach about gay people, so I knew the minute my sexuality came to light, they would remove my leadership responsibilities and take away my platform and my ability to do what I love. I was very fearful of that. I never again wanted to give people that level of power that was held over me when I was molested just because I wanted to belong or feel special. I came to understand very early on that I was determined to survive, regardless of what somebody might use to gain power over me.

STRIPPED OF POWER, BUT NOT PURPOSE

I was running a youth prayer group that started in the early evening and lasted until around ten at night. Our purpose was to pray for other young people around the country. We were able to bring young people from all over New Jersey to come together on Friday night—imagine that!—to pray for our communities and for young people who were under spiritual attack or suffering.

When I walked into the ministry one day, ready to start a prayer session, one of the pastors called me into the office to inform me that they would be canceling my youth prayer groups until further notice. I knew what it was about. A teenage kid of someone in church leadership had been acting out of the bounds of church protocol, and it had caused ripples of rumors and disappointment throughout the church. Even though I had nothing to do with the situation, it was decided it was best to stop all youth gatherings until further notice.

One Sunday, our senior pastor made a comment during a sermon to the whole congregation. He was preaching the house down, as he normally would do on a packed Sunday morning. And somewhere amidst calling out sins, he suddenly blurted out: "Sissies won't be looking at him in the bathroom. There is no place in the church for that!" And then he went on about how that would not be tolerated. It totally wounded me and humiliated me to hear a man I had looked to as a representative of God and a father figure use that word.

I was in shock and dumbfounded. To me, "sissy" meant "fag." Here was this man who I knew loved me, whom I had great admiration and love for. But to hear him speak like that—condemning people like me—and using a word that had been used against me so many times, brought me back to that place of not feeling safe. Suddenly, I felt as if my eyes were truly opened. It was as if a flashing red *beware* sign flashed across my mind. "Beware: he is only human, too." I no longer felt as safe, as protected, or valued.

The minute he used that word, "sissy," it stripped away every pedestal a young boy would put his father on. I said to myself, *That is not the God I know.*

Despite the inner turmoil I felt from the church leader's stance, I didn't understand that God was molding me into a better person.

During this time, my mom had started to clean the church during the day and the Newark courthouse at night, and she often assigned me bathroom duties. She instilled a strong work ethic in me pretty early on. On one hand, I was happy to be cleaning bathrooms, sinks, and floors because I had heard so many stories about great people who "got started" by doing tasks just like that. And I was finally able to have a job and make money. So, to me, I was cleaning toilets today because God had something better planned for me tomorrow.

On the other hand, Latino people have traditionally played the cleaning role so long in society that the label sticks, and I realized it was not a label I was ready to wear. So, when other cleaning jobs were offered to me, I took them, but I soon realized that it wasn't a good fit for me. I was ready for something else, something that allowed me to tap into my leadership abilities while feeling safe and valued.

From left to right: Stanley Fisher, mentor; me; and Congressman Donald Payne Sr., U.S. representative for New Jersey's 10th congressional district

Grandma Virginia and me in Newark (1999)

CHAPTER 3

Leading a Double Life: Exploring My Secret Identity

"Your individuality is important, but so is belonging.
Recognize the parts of your culture that have shaped your past,
and the parts you want to carry with you into the future."

—SOL PERALTA, AUDIENCE ENGAGEMENT MANAGER AT JOPWELL

At sixteen, after many weekends of babysitting and cleaning, I was ready for a new opportunity. I felt fortunate to be interviewing for a real office job at a nonprofit, a small community-based organization in Newark.

I had known about this organization since my childhood years. My mom's younger sister, Wanda, was the founder's first assistant, who had supported the staff since the start of the organization. She called me when the founder was looking for fresh new talent who could help with community engagement and fundraising.

The interview was with the founder of the North Jersey Community Research Initiative (NJCRI), Bill Orr, a man I had come to know when I was just nine years old when I delivered my grandmother's homemade lunches to him and my aunt. Even though he knew who I was and where I'd come from, it was by no means an easy interview. Looking back now, I realized I was tapping into the confidence and the many lessons my mentor, Stanley, and my church experiences had taught me. Before I walked in, I repeated these words in my head: *Believe in yourself. Know your worth. Speak with purpose. And if you don't know, just say you don't know!*

I had zero years of experience in community-based work and absolutely no idea what was in store for me. Bill warmly welcomed me in, offered me a seat at the small circular table in the corner of his office, and offered me a coffee, which I didn't drink at the time, but accepted. He took his seat and began asking away. He listened to my answers with a curious look in his eyes, which made me feel heard and seen. He did this by allowing me space to express my ideas and speak on the matters I was learning about, and also by encouraging me to speak when I felt moved to. Most importantly, he could communicate his vision clearly, creating a picture of what the organization was going to become—and the role I would play, if hired. I walked in wanting a job and walked out wanting to learn as much as I could about him.

After the interview, I was home undressing and hanging up my "good clothes" for another possible interview. That was when Bill called to tell me I'd gotten the job! They wanted to hire me to fundraise with him directly and work with my aunt on community events. I was overcome with joy. Here I was, just sixteen years old, and I'd just been offered a professional job in an office.

What was memorable about Bill was that he was decisive. He made informed decisions and stuck by them. He was a visionary, able to see possibilities others could not. He was demanding, yet kind and considerate. He was passionate, yet patient. He allowed mistakes to be a part of the learning process.

* * *

Needless to say, my way to celebrate was to get my CD player ready, head to the train, and sneak away for a night of wandering bliss, to a place where there were many others like me.

CHRISTOPHER STREET

I had first heard about Christopher Street as a young boy when my mom and stepdad would take us into New York on the PATH train to visit Central Park for the holidays. On those trips, the PATH final stop would be 34th Street. Every time we reached the Christopher Street train stop, my stepdad would nod in the direction of all the artistic-looking guys rushing off the train.

"You see them?" he'd say to my mom. "This stop is where all the gays go to work and hang out." He would explain how Christopher Street was filled with all sorts of creatives, musicians, men who dressed like women called drag queens, and people who could be themselves and not worry about getting beat up or hurt. He never had anything bad to say about them, just that consistent reminder and matter-of-fact bit of information he shared on every trip.

I still remember the first day I jumped on the train and got off at Christopher Street. As I nervously walked up the stairs, an energetic warm breeze pulled me up through the tunnel. Suddenly, I was in the Village at the Christopher Street Station.

I immediately felt its allure. Right in front of me, out in the open, all these gay men and trans women were walking up and down the street. Everything stopped, the world went silent, and for that moment, I felt like everyone was staring at me. I literally got dizzy because of the energy and eyes piercing right through me.

Did everyone sense my Village virginity? I imagined they were secretly whispering to each other, "That little Puerto Rican ain't from around here, girl." The moment all of those eyes looked at me, it was both terrifying and exhilarating. I thought, *This is where the other Black and Brown boys like me are!* I was petrified, but I felt like it was where I belonged. I was being seen.

Now, after the successful interview with Bill, I steadied myself at the top of the subway stairs. Today, I promised myself, to celebrate, I was going to try something new—I would go to a place called The Pier, a notorious spot at the end of Christopher Street. I saw quite a few people walking in one direction, and I reasoned that The Pier must be that way, too, so I followed.

On the way, I took it all in—so many different types of gay men together with their friends, in tight groups and cliques. But I was happy simply walking around the streets with my CD player, looking at all these unique people who looked so happy and carefree. I stared at couples holding hands or eating at outdoor cafes or restaurants. I saw men dressed as women and women dressed as men of all sizes and fashions proudly showcasing who they were, smiling, happy and laughing. My heart raced and body shook as I reacted with excitement, nervousness, and fear.

I had never seen anything like it before. If moving from the projects was like landing on another world, this was like landing in another galaxy. But I was ready. I had some acquired tools now and I was determined to become familiar with what seemed to be a safe space to spend my time exploring.

CAUGHT BETWEEN THE PIER AND THE PULPIT

The Pier, at that time, was literally deteriorating wooden planks and metal that stretched out into the Hudson River. It's been completely renovated since then. In the eighties and nineties, it was a gritty place to meet up with your friends, drink, hook up, or simply pass the time because you had nowhere else to go. For a lot of LGBTQIA+ young people, it was the only safe space in the city for us to be. Being so new to all of this, it took a lot of courage for me to even go to The Pier that first night.

I sat by myself off to the corner to people-watch. It was a beautiful summer night, yet chilled by the river winds. Even though I was cold, I couldn't think of leaving. I spent hours that first night watching groups of gay people come and go, dance and vogue, play music, and laugh. They all looked so different. As it got later and I began to lose my fight with time, I was ready to head out to catch the train. As my luck would have it, a sexy Spanish guy rolled by on rollerblades. He had tan skin, a buzz cut, tattoos down one arm, and wore a white tank top and blue basketball shorts with no underwear, which was evident as he moved.

I figured I caught his eye; he did a double take as he rolled by, then turned around and skated back toward me. "I'm Jose," he said in between breaths and as he tried to be cool, stopping his blades inches from me.

Great. Jose was the name I was going to use, I quickly thought. "I'm Julio," I said hesitantly. We talked for a few hours that night. He knew I was new to the scene and gave me plenty of advice, understanding from my 1,001 questions that I was naïve but so curious. I was happy to have an open conversation with someone who shared my experience, especially someone who looked as good as he did.

While we chatted, people around us smoked weed, some folks slept, and I witnessed for the first time somebody performing oral sex in public. I quickly learned that these sorts of things occurred all the time on The Pier, all the way until about five or six o'clock in the morning. Mr. Rollerblades offered to walk me to the train station and gave me his number. I swore I would see him again, but I never did.

After a few visits to Christopher Street, I became more and more comfortable with flirting and starting random conversations, which lead to many interesting and memorable interactions. This newfound comfort level and confidence allowed me to meet Andy Rodriguez, a Dominican kid carrying a silver and black boom box, wearing a durag at a pizza shop on 9th Street. With thick eyebrows, a short muscular build, and a Bronx Spanish accent, he looked like the typical Latino porn star found on endless VHS covers showcased in the windows of gay sex shops. This led to me being invited to hang out on Christopher Street, and later with three of his friends, Andrew, Junior, and Kay—all cute Black and Latino gay boys. While all his friends flirted with anyone walking by all night, Andy was the only one in the group who had caught my eye.

The previous month, I had been sitting in a church assisting pastors. The next month, I was sitting on a step stool next to a gay bar and a sex shop in New York City, hoping no one I knew walked by…but also caring less and less if they did.

I hadn't known Andy and his friends for long, but after about my first three hours of chilling with them, I felt a connection and a strong sense of family. Over the course of the next month, they became my new family. Whether they were introducing me to everyone as their little brother, buying me food, or making sure I had money to get on the train back home, they seemed to genuinely care about me. They didn't have a lot, but they always shared the little they had and made sure I felt included. If I stayed quiet too long or fell back, they quickly brought me back into the conversation. They always made me believe I mattered by including me in the decisions for the day.

From my visits into the Village, I learned that all of them were sex workers, homeless, and staying at a local LGBTQIA+ shelter. Even though I knew this, it didn't matter to me. This sense of brotherhood created a safe space, and if they were willing to include me, I was down. This was the first time I looked at family differently from what I believed it should look like. It was so far from the traditional Puerto Rican household I was used to, and far from the pictures that the church ingrained in me. It was my chosen family—not perfect, but my new safe space.

I quickly learned that every day can be a party on Christopher Street. Safe spaces were created often there and made for the celebration of life and of each other. And when I say every day, I am not exaggerating. There was literally a party at specific clubs and bars every day: Monsters on Monday, The Stone Wall on Tuesday, Heavens on Wednesday, Chi Chiz on Thursday, The Cock Ring on Friday, The Tunnel on Saturday, and the infamous but mandatory Limelight on Sunday.

As I adapted and attempted to thrive in this new world, I could have never guessed that the Village, just like the Newark Project, would play a central part in my story.

FINALLY ON THE RIGHT PATH

I was nervous as I prepared for the first day of my new job. Working with the founder and creator of an organization for your first professional job is intimidating. My aunt Wanda played a vital role in teaching me and correcting my mistakes, and she was my go-to for everything. In fact, she had played a vital role in me entering LGBTQIA+ work to begin with.

Months earlier, she had invited me to attend a "focus group" at the agency, where members of the community were asked questions and provided feedback. I had no idea at the time that it involved the LGBTQIA+ community.

When I showed up for the focus group, I was met by a super happy, excited, and cute eighteen-year-old, Thishin, and an inquisitive and detailed nineteen-year-old, Shelton, who made it a point to introduce me to the group. The meeting was being led by a more somber, serious-looking middle-aged Black man, Frank Martin, a former Rutgers University biologist. When I walked in, they were in deep, passionate conversation about the HIV epidemic and the high rates of infections they were seeing in Newark in Black and Latino gay and bisexual men.

I was shocked that my aunt had referred me to this group as I hadn't come out to her, or to anyone, yet. But it was both exciting and eye-opening to witness the passion on an issue in the gay community that I wasn't even aware of at the time.

The Community Advisory Group, as we were called, was trying to figure out what the Black and Latinx gay community wanted and needed in terms of support. Once they compiled that information, the group could use it to inform our planning and program designing. During the focus group, they asked all sorts of questions, like, "If you were to name the project, what would you call it?"

"How can services be delivered?"

"What hours would the project operate?"

"How could we do outreach and identify other Black and Brown gay men to engage?"

They specifically asked us those questions, seeking information on how best to reach and support gay men who were on the down low, meaning men who identified publicly as heterosexual but were discreetly having sex with men. The group of men expressed the need for an LGBTQIA+ center in Newark because there were no designated LGBTQIA+ safe spaces at that time. The New Jersey organizations we know of today as LGBTQIA+ safe spaces simply did not exist back in 1998.

In witnessing this discussion of the HIV epidemic, I become conscious that gay sex carried with it a certain risk, and realized how it affected Black gay men differently from white gay men. At that time, for every hundred people tested for HIV on mobile testing units in the city, there were two to three positive results a week.

The organization applied for a CDC demonstration grant, which serviced at-risk young men who have sex with men, and from that application and award, the Project WOW (Web Outreach Works) LGBTQIA+ center emerged. We got funded a year into my new position of working with the founder. Soon after, I became an official full-time team member and an integral part of the Project WOW center.

EARLY DAYS AT THE LGBTQIA+ CENTER

That somber-looking Black man in the back of the room coordinating and listening to our discussion ended up being my first manager. I learned in time that he was friendly, and yet very serious whenever it came to anything related to HIV programming or community organizing. His questions were sharp, and at random moments, he would test us by having us reteach material we'd just learned back to him or to others. He created a culture of preparedness, and I made sure I was always ready to meet or exceed his expectations.

Looking back, I now know he was making sure he created a standard for us to follow. He wanted to be assured that no one was "playing games with his time," as he would often say, and that no one dared play games with ours.

The second manager, Amistad St. Aromand, was a brilliant, courageous twenty-eight-year-old Haitian man who had an infectious laugh and beautiful attitude. He used his story to show and tell people what HIV and AIDS looked like by fearlessly disclosing his own AIDS status.

He challenged people's stereotypical ideas on what it was like to live with HIV or what HIV looked like in a person. And the most impactful thing he did for our teams, both personally and professionally, was to mentor us about being a fair human and leader. He took every chance and challenge that came our way to show us that he was not only our boss, but that he was also our brother in this fight.

Time and time again, he told me, "Julio, I am your brother in this. I am your manager when I need to be, but in the community and in the field, I am your brother in the struggle, and I am going to hold you responsible and to a higher standard than just a worker."

He developed me. He challenged me. And he provided me guidance and corrections to my mistakes by calling them out as they occurred. He expected accountability, and I respected that.

He could have fired me for my failures, but just as some had done in the past, he showed me grace and concessions instead. He looked past what was boiling at the surface and saw what was budding at my core. He knew that I had the talent and work ethic it was going to take to bring young at-risk Black and Brown people into Project WOW, but he also understood that I was young, still developing, and finding myself.

It was definitely a balancing act. Yet he allowed me to grow and make mistakes with a lot of compassion and wisdom on his end. When you find these types of mentors, do not let them go.

LEADING WITH COURAGE

"HIV LOOKS" was all I could make out of the words on his shirt as he shouted at the top of his lungs through the noise of the thousands of people in the exhibit hall. "JULIO!" he called out to me. As he approached, the words got bigger on his crisp, clean white T-shirt in red bold letters: "THIS IS WHAT HIV LOOKS LIKE." I knew who he was, although I couldn't remember his name. His face was vaguely familiar, but his energy wasn't missing a beat. I had met him a year prior working a booth at the Javits Jacob Center for NYC Pride weekend when he was representing an organization attempting to give me condoms and lubes, and not accepting no as an answer. His humor and persistence wore me down.

"Hey, Julio! I'm Marco, Marco Benjamin. Do you remember me?" he smiled.

"Of course, I do!" I responded with a relieved smile back. (Thank God he told me his name.) "What are you doing here?"

"I'm here this year at USCA [United States Conference on HIV/AIDS] to protest the high prices of HIV medications targeting and limiting access for Black and Brown communities affected by the virus. I'm also organizing a protest in this same exhibit hall! We have to do something, Julio, and let these companies know we will not take this laying down, that this cannot continue!" I agreed with him and felt his passion.

"I totally understand. Is that why you got that shirt on?"

"NO! I got this shirt on to address the stigma of HIV and fear many have in sharing their status. I wanted to place a face on it." There was absolutely no shame in his voice or in his expression, and I admired that.

"That's incredible! I'm so honored to know people like you," I said.

"Join us, please! We need every voice," he pleaded.

I instantly felt nervous. "Me? Protest? I have a meeting later. I'm so sorry!" I lied.

I really didn't have a meeting, but I was prepared to say anything to *not go*. And I was terrified of disrupting any conference activity. I didn't want to stand out, and it was more comfortable to watch. After all, at least *someone* was doing it. Who was he to put me on the spot like that? I didn't plan for this. I didn't clear it with my agency. I knew nothing about the HIV drug price increase. I didn't even know the time or location, so even if I changed my mind, I couldn't go. Fear was setting in, and stepping out had me feeling all kinds of ways, to the point where I took Marco's well-intended invitation and almost turned it into an insult. I had to check myself for a moment and ask myself why I was being triggered this way.

Here Marco was taking on the stigma of HIV by owning it and sharing his story, seeing what he believed was an injustice and taking action. He took action any way he knew how with the resources he had, including people, T-shirts, signs, and sheer will. He decided when and where he would act: at the USCA. He understood he had to lead by taking responsibility and weathering any negative consequence. And he was doing what he asked of others himself first.

His group of protesters became the talk of the conference and sparked conversations that needed to take place on all levels of drug pricing and access. The following year, the conference format was changed to bring greater attention to the issues of drug price increases raised by his actions.

When we talk about leadership, it's crucial to think about what it means to lead with courage. But not the sort of courage it takes to run toward a fire, fight off a gang of wrongdoers, block a barrage of bullets, or what any Avenger movie tells us is heroic and brave.

No, I'm talking about the courage it takes to use your own experiences to help others live in their own truths. Your experiences and stories of hope, triumph, struggles, and trauma, if shared, can enlighten a community. This courage is often more difficult than fighting off fear because it requires us to be vulnerable, to make visible our scars, and to amplify what frightens us the most. It takes a lot of trust—in yourself and those around you—to lead with this type of courage.

I learned I was going to need courage early on. Frank Martin, the manager of the Project WOW center, had a habit of having his staff randomly do teach-backs about what we learned in our state trainings. He would publicly challenge us to defend our arguments in community meetings by asking thoughtful and more in-depth questions. Questions I had to stop and think about in the moment. I hated being put on the spot, mostly because it terrified me. But also, I felt like I couldn't get comfortable in public with him around because I was always a little on edge. I always had to be prepared to share something.

Many days, I resented him for it because of how uncomfortable it made me. Looking back now, I see how this was preparing us and keeping us on our toes so we would always be courageous enough and be ready to communicate truth to power. Frank understood the power of information and awareness. He understood that the more we knew, the more confident we would become, thus allowing us to advocate for ourselves and our community more courageously. He had many conversations with me about how people will also use or withhold information to withhold power. And so being informed of truth and facts was key to balancing that scale of power others have concentrated for themselves or who they believe should share in it.

Very few of us are born heroes. And life isn't a superhero movie or a page in a comic book. So where does this courage come from? Do we find it by acting tough? Not at all. Do we find it while being a know-it-all? Nope. Being a truly brave leader comes from taking action and responsibility for the good and bad. It means pushing your own ego aside and instead focusing on the goals of your community and supporting the needs of those you are leading. With practice, if you lead with those values, you'll become a courageous leader.

Here's what I mean:

- **Take action:** "If you're required to do it, I should also be willing to do it" is an incredibly powerful motivator. By walking the walk and talking the talk, you will avoid the dreaded trap that destroys a leader's reputation: hypocrisy. Action is what inspires the "if I can do it, so can you" attitude.

- **Be decisive:** The number one obstacle to success is a leader's failure to make a hard decision. Courageous leaders don't hesitate. They use the facts, consult the data, push away the doubt, and trust their gut. The hard truth is that, yes, taking action can result in a negative outcome, but delaying a decision will only ever have negative consequences.

- **Take responsibility:** Being a leader doesn't mean telling others what to do or throwing folks under the bus, and it certainly doesn't mean taking all the credit when it ends well. Being a leader means taking responsibility for the team and supporting them so they can do their best work. It means making decisions knowing that you'll be the one who will deal with the consequences.

- **Maintain your composure:** When things go south—and they will sometimes go south—there will be no throwing cell phones or other objects across the office, no yelling at subordinates, and no slamming doors. It's crucial to keep it together and stay calm in a crisis and set a stoic example for your team to prevent them from panicking.

These qualities are just a few of many. But listing these qualities is important to highlight the fact that we already display these characteristics, and many of us live them every single day.

*   *   *

In the late 1990s and early 2000s, we began establishing policies and procedures for delivering support services online to the LGBTQIA+ community. Which hadn't been done throughout the whole country. Needless to say, there was a lot of trial and error and too many unknowns to count, since we were on the cutting edge of this type of work. We traveled all over the country, as eighteen- and nineteen-year-olds, teaching other organizations and LGBTQIA+ leaders how to do web and internet outreach. We shared our best practices for delivering online programs for at-risk LGBTQIA+ youth. In the process, we quickly found out just how many Black and Latinx LGBTQIA+ people needed anonymous, confidential, and nonjudgmental support from a trained individual in a safe space.

NEW YORK RAVEN—A NEW SAFE SPACE. KIND OF

Since the internet was still in its infancy at that time, our group started community outreach with local phone chatlines. Meeting guys online was not possible for everyone yet; even if it was, not everyone in the inner city had access to computers, cable, and a subscription service all at once. Back then, when the computer started making its way into every home, Gateway was the primary computer of choice, and you needed internet access—a luxury for most of us back then—and an internet service to get you online, like the infamous AOL dial-up. Because of that limitation and lack of access period, we turned to the next best thing; chat phone lines as our place to meet other gay guys looking for fun.

The biggest chatline at the time was called the "New York Raven." It serviced five different areas: Manhattan, Queens, Brooklyn, the Bronx, and Northern NJ. I had learned about the chatlines through my friend, Kina. She was a funny, huge-hearted girl two years older than me who had befriended me on the steps of my building. She was so free-spirited and was one of the three people I first confided in about *the real me*. She lived across the street with her younger sister, and the easy access almost guaranteed a hang out every day. I joined chatlines, learned about them with her, and listened to these guys tell her what they wanted to do, what they were working with sexually, and all that other exciting... THOT stuff.

Naturally, I became curious. The moment I got away, I called that same line that Kina had called. I didn't realize there were "M for M" (men for men) and "W for W" sections. I was so inexperienced to this lifestyle that it still did not click with me that of course they would delineate. But once I called in and heard it was an option, I pressed the number three, M for M, and that was that. I was hooked; I started calling it every single day.

The initial feature of the chatlines was live rooms. There might be ten rooms, with around ten guys in every room just talking, joking, killing time, and really just having light-hearted conversations. Then, you'd go on to the next room and another ten guys. Everybody would create a different persona, a fake name. Mine was "VIP," so I usually entered the room with, "Yo, VIP's on the line. What's goin' on, guys?" I had a very deep voice, and it created many fans from the start. The requests to go to private rooms for one-on-one talks were endless. I spent hours on the line, imagining what the faces behind the sexy voices looked like. This only increased my desire from wanting to chat on the phone to meet in person.

These live chat rooms were where I first learned about the easily accessible world of sex work or simply "getting a date." If you were young and you wanted to make money, you would simply leave a public message. Many down-low men went on the phone chatlines to pick up young men or offer money for sex anonymously. I learned early that the downtown or uptown men were the ones to chat with, since that was where the financial districts were. I was curious, of course, by the stories of easy money, but told myself I'd never do sex work.

The second feature of the chatlines was the mailbox feature. If you didn't want to be a part of the live groups, a sultry man's voice would say, "For you shy boys, if you don't want to be in the main rooms with everyone else, press two now." This section was similar to the personal ads in the newspapers. You would go there to record a message for others to hear and respond to. Mine might be: "Hey, what's up? My name is VIP. I'm a 5'11" Puerto Rican. I'm 170 pounds and from North Newark. I'm a top and I'm looking to date. Please leave me a message with your age, location, and full description if you're interested." It was that simple.

A few hours or days later, I checked my voicemail to hear all the messages that guys had left, along with their phone numbers. I had the option of sending them a message back or deleting them. That was how we found each other when not traveling to NYC or a local cruising spot.

The phone chatline was also how I met my first boyfriend, Aaron. He sounded cool over the phone, and when we finally met up at KFC on Park Avenue, I was not disappointed. (Note: we did not eat Kentucky Fried Chicken that night.) He was confident and funny, with a background in the church since childhood, just like me. Our meetup was the start of a five-year relationship, a journey into the heart of the gay lifestyle, and discovering my truth. Finally.

MY FIRST BOYFRIEND

After meeting my first boyfriend over the chatline, there was no going back for me. I had just turned eighteen, and it finally felt like my real life was beginning. I went to his house for the first time on the first night I met him, and I never really left. There were already five other people living there in a two-bedroom apartment. They were all young Puerto Ricans, gay or trans, and all entertainers or working in the club scene. Together, they had built this family structure. I could see they all felt safe, were happy with this world, and content with the family unit they'd built around themselves.

There was Alex, otherwise known as Alexa Monroe, a drag performer; Maria, the mother figure, a beautiful and stunning transgender woman who was an amazingly talented nail artist; Junior, the father figure, a shortly built barber, hairstylist, and dressmaker; and David, the youngest, who was a line cook during the week and Frangelica Monroe on weekends. Finally, Aaron worked at a bank and played piano as a side gig at parties or bars. They all had unique, vibrant personalities and expressed themselves with a freedom and fearlessness I had never known.

Junior and Maria were the oldest members of the group. They worked and budgeted and always made sure the household did not go without. Alex and David were the younger members. So, when I came into the picture, I was the new guy that their gay uncle Aaron was dating.

After about two weeks of staying there, the whole family sat me down and invited me to stay. Maria and Junior went over the house rules, dos and don'ts, and how budgeting would work. They showed me how to live in a group where I didn't have to consistently hide my behavior or expression, and I was finally accepted into my first LGBTQIA+ chosen family. Everybody took me under their wing. Each of them showed me what it was to be gay, free, and proud, and also what it meant to be your unique self. I'd never had that kind of fearlessness in my life before, and I was hungry for more of it.

At this point, I was coming to full terms with my lifestyle and who I was, and it was a little chaotic. Every day I was doing this amazing work at the LGBTQIA+ center, and every night we visited Christopher Street in The Village.

I was never into the drugs that kept you chasing a high, like crack, dope, or crystal meth. Instead, I drank like a fish, smoked tons of pot, and popped ecstasy as part of the admission process at clubs. I partied for maybe two or three years with pills, until a sudden increase in deaths scared me when several friends overdosed on other drugs. The deaths made taking drugs a little darker, but it was a darkness that my friends and I were still willing to dabble in.

The drug and club scene can become a dangerous combination if left unchecked. I have personally witnessed friends lose it all because the partying outweighed everything they had worked so hard to achieve and create.

Looking back, as dangerous and risky as the party life was, it was also the most amazing time of my life. I was eighteen and really trying to find out who I was and who I was not. I was finding my voice. I became comfortable with being unapologetically me within the spaces I created for myself. The one thing I hadn't gotten comfortable with was being fully seen by my blood family.

TIME TO ASK FOR HELP

I didn't know how to have that conversation with my mom about my boyfriend and new living situation, so I didn't have any conversation at all. My mom spent most of her days in church, and we barely saw each other, so I ghosted her for about six months. I stopped all communication with most of my family during this time. It was a period all about discovering myself—at least, that's what I told myself—and my new boyfriend, my new chosen family, and the new LGBTQIA+ life I had entered.

Looking back now, I realize I could have handled the situation differently. Today, I understand that to live as your true self, you must be courageous and hold yourself accountable. But back then, I was unreachable by choice while still living in the same city as my mom. A choice that put her through Hell.

One night, Aaron and I got into a really bad argument. We were still getting to know each other, and he'd been living with this group of people he had already known for years. I'd only been there for a few months, and there were clashes about boundaries and respect, and my zero tolerance for his flirting with other people. I was all about going out, partying, and doing whatever he wanted with our friends. But going out and not coming home was never going to be acceptable.

It wasn't an argument I was expecting to win, nor one on which we were willing to compromise, so I told him I was out. I would just move back in with my mom, a lie I delivered with pride. I was also embarrassed that I had cut off my relationship with my mom, and I felt that I *couldn't* go back to her house. With my pride holding me back and nowhere else to go, I wound up sleeping on the street, in random motel rooms, and on people's couches for months.

I still had to go to work every day, so most days I went to work exhausted and hungry. I often served our clients food, packing leftovers to eat once I left work. I certainly wasn't going to tell the center or my job that I needed help. I wanted to make sure I was never looked at as a client myself, in need of basic help. There goes my pride again.

Before and after work, while it was still dark, I'd sit on a bench at the park, listening to my headphones and trying to stay as awake and alert as I could. Nighttime became a dreadful experience for me, because even though I was exhausted, I needed to stay up to protect myself and be alert. Without fail, the adrenaline would wear off at some point, and I'd fall asleep. At the start of each morning, I was already dreading the evening.

I had allowed my pride to get in the way of just asking for help. What I realized is, although I did have several places I could have gone—my mom's apartment being one, and my aunt's house being another—I *felt* like I didn't have anywhere to go. There were no safe spaces for me, much less a place where a *provider like me* could go for help without running into someone I worked with, or a client I provided services to. I felt a mix of shame and frustration because I was the one who was supposed to have it all together so I could help others, and there I was, homeless, unable but mostly unwilling to reach out and help myself.

It didn't have to be that way, but I was too young (if youth is an excuse) and stubborn to go home. I knew I did not want to be placed back in that closed box I had just escaped, so if that meant being homeless or hooking up with someone, then I resolved to do what was needed to survive.

I couch-surfed whenever possible, for one day here or there, but I never wanted to be a burden and wear out my welcome. My aunt Dolly had been one of my best friends growing up, and she let me wash clothes at her house and take showers there. A lot of people I stayed with were working people, so I was conscious of things like food and consumption of their supplies, other people's privacy, and not overstepping my boundaries, because I knew that their kindness could and would run out. I was always aware of how to be tolerable in other people's spaces, a lesson I had learned early on. Thankfully, I had friends in the community who were lifesavers in helping me navigate that period of my life.

Being exposed every night, both physically and emotionally, was making me feel worthless. I felt like less of a human by the stares I received from people who assumed I was an unemployed homeless person. All of these things made me go back to my boyfriend, Aaron, to try to make that situation work, whether I should have or not. But I really missed my family.

When I think about all of the emotions I carried around with me during that time, it was probably one of the darkest places I've been, mostly because it was one of the most isolated.

I needed hope. I needed help.

And even though I was a legal adult, I needed my mom.

CHAPTER 4

Coming Out to My Mother

"Acknowledge and embrace the person you are,
imperfections and all. That's the highest service we can achieve:
to give back and give to ourselves in the best way we know."

**—DR. PAUL BONIN RODRIGUEZ, ASSISTANT PROFESSOR
AT THE UNIVERSITY OF TEXAS, AUSTIN**

About a year after I'd moved away from home, I was at the center, working and thinking about my mom as I so often did. With the church only three city blocks from me, I couldn't help but compare how different the world was in those three blocks. My thoughts were occasionally interrupted as I overheard a team member counsel a person who was asking for advice about coming out to his mom.

Toward the end of the conversation, the team member confirmed what I was piecing together: "So it seems like today is the day you're going to tell your mom." In this moment, a sense of peace flowed through my entire body, and I knew what I had to do next.

MY MOM, THE MAIL, AND A HOLY MOMENT IN THE SANCTUARY

My boyfriend and I resolved our argument, I moved back in with him, and we coasted along for the next year and a half. I was back to the grind of working, in a relationship, and heading into the city with my roommates every night to Limelight, Roxy, The Tunnel, Karsh in Queens, and Heaven. I also had what they called the John Blair VIP card, which could get you into certain after-hours locations and clubs.

I knew I needed to make things right with my mom, but I just didn't know how to start the process after all this time. I was scared and embarrassed that I had no reasonable excuse as to why I disappeared. As it turned out, I was about to get a little help from the postal service.

My mom had been assuming more leadership roles in the church and studying for her bachelor's degree in religious education, while she was still doing her facility work. As a part of her education progress, she was invited to teach her first message to the whole church. She excitingly called my job to invite me to attend, and I accepted.

Maybe this was my opportunity to tell her. I cannot describe the extent of my nervousness as I walked into church, into the same sanctuary that I had once prayed in, preached in, and laid hands in, to now listen to my mother teach the Word of God. She did a wonderful job, but I wasn't able to focus on what she was saying, both because of the butterflies inside me and because I was rehearsing what I was going to say to her, hoping she didn't react badly.

After all the churchgoers had left, I hung around to wait for her in the now-darkened sanctuary. With only the dim lights on the stage that highlighted the crystal pulpit, it felt especially holy.

Today was her day, I told myself. *She has worked so hard. I can't come out today and ruin her day.* With slight relief, I breathed in and repeated mentally, *Not today.*

My mom walked over to me, her eyes filled with tears, and she gave me a big hug, saying she missed me.

"How'd I do?" she asked shyly.

I told her how proud I was of her hard work and staying with it, and that I was sorry for being gone. In response, she told me she loved me and asked, "Is there anything you want to tell me or anything you want to talk to me about?"

I thought, *She must know. She must be angry. She must be devastated. I can't tell her now. We're in church!*

So I lied and said, "No." I certainly wasn't going to tell my mom that I was gay while standing in the sanctuary.

She pulled a red envelope from her purse, and the famous John Blair symbol on the corner of the envelope caught my eye. I started panicking. *Oh, my God. Oh, my God. Oh, my God.* I instantly realized my mistake. When I signed up for my VIP card, the one that could get me into after-hours gay clubs, I'd absentmindedly written down her home address.

She asked, "Can you tell me about this, Julio?" and handed me a small stack of promo cards. The picture on the front of the first promo card was from an Angel and Devil Halloween party and featured strippers in wings and thongs.

I remember thinking, *Really, Julio? Angels and Devils? Of all the postcards for parties to open at church. See, God does have a sense of humor, okay?*

To try to soften the blow, and realizing the ruse was up, I finally said, "Mom, I do have something to tell you. I have been in a relationship for two years. I love him and didn't know how to tell you."

In her next breath, she began to apologize profusely to me when I thought *I* was going to be the only one apologizing. I guess a mother's heart always knows. And I think in those moments, she finally connected the dots of why I stayed away so long.

With tears now falling down her cheeks, my mother looked at me lovingly and said, "Julio, I love you so much. You will always be my son. We grew up together in a way. I know now how unfair it was to you. You were always my old man." She always used that term with me because I was wise and mature beyond my years. "I don't care what you are doing now or who you love, but you can't stay away from me like that anymore. I'm your mother and always will be. You come first to me. I love you more than anything."

I'd left home to live a secret life, believing that my mother wouldn't approve of who I was. I'd run away from her because I didn't think she could give me the safety to be myself. I was so wrong.

I knew her tears were a mixture of acceptance and the realization that I had been carrying this heavy burden on my own for so long. She just cried and cried in front of me, and I resisted every urge inside me to apologize for being gay.

I didn't have to apologize, though. She told me she loved me. She would never, ever judge me, and she would always be there for me. What a relief! Finally admitting to my mom that I loved someone—that he made me feel special and he loved me—was the most liberating thing in the world for me. Her reaction was so unconditional, just like every child hopes for. It was not a horror story like I'd heard from so many other LGBTQIA+ people. Even in that moment, I was very aware then that this was a privilege not many of my LGBTQIA+ siblings ever experienced.

I was blessed to have a mother who loved me beyond her understanding or comforts. It haunted me afterward for some time that I had put my mom through so much during my journey of trying to get to know the real me. She was, and is, my angel.

As I write these words, I am reminded of how amazing God is. God showed me that I can be *who* I am, *wherever* I am. He said, "You are going to come out to your mom here in church where you once felt safe. I want you to feel safe again."

Looking back, that was purposeful. God orchestrated that to show me that He loves me still, and that being gay did not mean that I was condemned to a hopeless place.

That night, God became a safe space for me again. And my mother loved me unconditionally.

Now, I could begin to heal.

LOUD AND PROUD

After I came out to my mom, I didn't care who else knew. Before that day, I had always lived a very compartmentalized life. What I did at work, stayed at work. What I did in New York, stayed in New York. What I did with my family, stayed with my family. Until that point, they had always been totally separate things. But not anymore.

Six months after getting back with my boyfriend, we realized living in a house with four other single people was not good for our relationship, so we moved into a one-bedroom apartment together right down the block.

My twin brother probably always knew I was gay, and I don't think it was ever an issue with him. As a kid, I'm sure he didn't love having such a different brother because all the kids made fun of that sort of thing, but he was always ready to fight and defend me, much like my uncles. Angel always had the biggest heart, and he never made me feel bad about myself, regardless of how I acted or whom I chose to hang out with.

Then, there were the uncles. They'd protected me from being bullied for being different in the projects, but I wasn't sure if they'd be cool with me being openly gay. That was going to be a hit-or-miss conversation. Regardless, I didn't have to wait long.

Franky, one of my roughest uncles, came over unannounced to the new place my boyfriend and I shared. As soon as he walked in, he outright asked me, "Are you and Aaron together? You don't have to lie to me, Julio."

With a mop in one hand, I stopped cleaning, looked at him for what felt like eternity, and said, "Yes, we're partners."

He said, "Julio, I don't care what you are. You're my nephew and I love you. Nobody better fuck with you. If you ever have an issue, you let me know." I laughed a little and breathed a sigh of relief.

I immediately felt better. If he knew and accepted that I was gay, I felt like telling anybody else would be a piece of cake.

So, I slowly started introducing my partner through my conversations. Over time, he integrated and blended right in to the family. I didn't introduce him as my partner until a little later, instead using the infamous line, "This is my friend."

They treated him like they treated me, with acceptance and love. It felt like they had been waiting for a long time for me to be comfortable enough to show them the real me. I felt like the luckiest person in the world.

My mom had missed me so much that she simply said, "I'm not going to do anything that will cause you to leave again." There was an adjustment period as she got used to me being gay. Initially, she tolerated my relationship with my partner. Quickly, however, she came to accept it fully, and then exceeded even my highest expectations to become the proud mom of a gay son and an ally to the LGBTQIA+ community in general. She's especially involved in supporting the trans community, and now she provides access to women's clothing, hygiene products, shoes, and more through church donations.

Today, she tries to walk in all of our LGBTQIA+ marches with us. She visits the local LGBTQIA+ centers, drops off food and clothes to the staff, and is the de facto mom to many of my gay friends. She walks beside me on my journey and stands with me in my truth.

PREACHING A NEW KIND OF SERMON

With my family on board, I was more excited than ever to make a difference in the LGBTQIA+ community. I was promoted from the full-time outreach position to a new full-time role as a health educator. In this role, I held groups and talks with young gay men and trans women on ways to keep themselves safe both sexually and physically. I also helped them identify triggers that put them at risk, utilize communication tools to advocate for themselves, build health literacy and education, and understand the impact of the HIV epidemic on people of color. This is how I went from student to teacher, and now was my time to be the voice in the room. I could barely contain my excitement!

The interesting thing was that while I was leading groups on a wide range of topics, like safe-sex practices and risk reduction regarding drug use, I was still learning from my own experiences and the community. I was delivering services and operating a safe space while still getting those "ah-ha" moments pertaining to my own life.

That just confirms a theory that I wholeheartedly believe in: You can be an advocate while needing and receiving advocacy yourself. You don't have to be perfect or have it all together. I certainly was not perfect then, and still am not perfect now, but I love what I do and I'm good at it.

THE IMPORTANCE OF PASSION

In my career, I've seen a lot of potential leaders who are stuck in unproductive cycles. They're making plan after plan, preparing for their opportunity, striving for perfection, patiently waiting for the right moment. I don't know who needs to hear this, but life is short, and it's perfectly okay to make mistakes and fail. Be passionate in your endeavors.

Passion is what propels you and drives you to make progress. Aligning your actions with your passion refuels you and defines your purpose. For example, I remember a time when it didn't matter how much sleep I got: I would drag myself out of bed. Even though I loved the work and I felt I was called to do it, the challenges I knew I'd face at work each day tired me out before the day even started. Whether I was working with community members, agency staff, managers, and directors who ran public health programming or creating safe spaces to save lives, these interactions and planning sessions could be a consistent form of stress at the forefront of my day. I knew something had to change. I loved what I was doing, yet I wasn't showing up in terms of my energy. They say that to do the same thing over and over and expect different results is the definition of insanity. So I decided to change it up a little.

Every morning before I opened my eyes, and before allowing the crashing thoughts and to-do lists of the day to take hold in my mind, I would thank God for a new day and for allowing me another morning of waking up. After I opened my eyes and stepped out of bed, I thanked God for allowing my feet to touch the floor, and for allowing me to see where they would take me. It took practice and a sense of awareness to shift my thinking and keep those crashing thoughts at bay, but I found that by waking up and being thankful for life, the gratitude that enters me shifts my mood and allows me to start getting excited for the tasks ahead. I still do this today, and it makes me feel enthusiastic about everything that I do. I become more deeply committed when I'm passionate, and I am resilient in the face of challenges.

Passion moves you forward with emotional connections. It opens your heart and allows you to view others with compassion.

When my spirit is low, I look beyond my emotions and use my powers of reason to reignite my passion. I do this by devoting myself to meaningful activities that make my dreams a reality.

If you're seeking a new passion in your own life, ask yourself:

1. What sparks my creativity?

2. What are three new activities that I always wanted to try?

3. How do I celebrate the passion that exists inside of me rather than seeking it in external sources?

* * *

I started realizing that my voice mattered, my body mattered, and my presence mattered. I was becoming the creator of my own experience while simultaneously advocating for the needs of my community.

It became blatantly obvious that there were not a lot of young LGBTQIA+ people of color who represented Latinxs in the field. As a health educator, part of the requirement was that I needed to be at the table serving as a vocal part of planning groups and committees. I also needed to represent my specific gay community: young Black and Latino gay men, as well as the LGBTQIA+ community at large.

I found myself now always wanting to be able to speak for the little guy, that shy Brown Latino boy. I always had to remind myself that I was the only gay Latino in the room a lot of the time. In essence, I was the little guy. Finally, this was a situation where that disparity came in handy and made my voice and perspective one of a kind!

It was definitely a challenge, but it also worked for me because it made me one of the only people in the room who could speak to the queer Latinxs' experience. It also gave me a platform that I could utilize to its fullest potential.

This was my church now. And I was going to give the best sermons week after week that I possibly could.

BEING AN ADVOCATE 24/7

Being an advocate means different things for different people. For me, being an advocate means being a resource, a bridge-builder, and a voice for those who can't or won't speak.

If I find that my community has a lack of resources, such as a lack of safe spaces, funding, or expertise, it is my job as an advocate to connect them with the resources to help them.

If you're an advocate, that doesn't mean doing it all on your own; it means partnering with a network of resources, where appropriate.

I haven't always seen myself as an advocate. When I first started doing community-based work and heard the word "advocate," my mind envisioned a person marching in Washington, DC, holding a sign, willing to tie themself to buildings and be arrested. To me, that was an advocate.

What I learned quickly is that anyone can be an advocate. And giving someone a platform is being an advocate.

Back then, every day after work, I headed to the city to have a great ol' time. Then, the next morning, I was back to work for my community. I didn't realize I was doing advocacy work then. Even more mind-blowing to me looking back is that I didn't understand that my shift as a community advocate didn't end at five o'clock. It was a twenty-four-hour-a-day job.

CONNECTING WITH YOUR COMMUNITY

For those interested in becoming advocates in a new community, my advice is to first get acquainted with your local community and look for resources like LGBTQIA+ centers or groups and ways to support them. Google does wonders these days. You likely only know a fraction of the resources available, and I hope there is a community waiting for you in your city or town!

If you are interested in becoming involved in your LGBTQIA+ community, here's how you start:

1. **Make a list of places you've heard about in your community but never visited.** Maybe your city has an LGBTQIA+ center that offers regular groups or social

activities. If you've never attended group activities, put that on your list. Gay bingo and movie nights at the park are my favorite! Many times, a calendar of events will be available online, allowing you to pick and choose how you want to get your feet wet. If you don't find something you're familiar with, try something new!

2. **Frequent your neighborhood hangout.** Whether it's the local coffee shop, a bookstore, or the grill cafe a few blocks away, find a relaxed place to support and connect with other community members. Truly connecting with your community involves getting out and meeting friends, old and new. It never hurts to check out reviews or look for signs of LGBTQIA+ friendliness on their website. We have allies in many places.

3. **Discover the freebies.** Free events and venues abound in many communities. Take advantage of everything free that your community has to offer, from public libraries and parks to nature sanctuaries, fairs, and pride events. I find that by supporting free local events, you are supporting amazing local organizations, towns, people, and cities that work to make it happen. Their success is often measured by community presence, so it means a lot.

4. **Visit your local museums.** Yes, I said it: museums! You'll have some fun and learn something fascinating about the community in which you live. Even the smallest towns often have a museum or two. For folks in small towns and big cities alike, this is a great way to explore beyond the boundaries of your local community and look for LGBTQIA+ influences.

5. **Consider your local tourist attractions.** There's a reason why people travel far and wide to come enjoy the tourist attractions in your area. Find out why! Even though you

might think tourist attractions aren't your thing, you don't know for sure what such venues offer until you experience them firsthand. Support others the way you'd like to be supported. Many local attractions depend on the dollars of visitors to stay open, to expand, or to just pay their staff. Support your local attractions and sites safely. Especially post-COVID.

6. **Take a notebook or use your phone's note app when you're out in your community.** When you're actively looking or exploring your community, you'll be surprised by how many local businesses and organizations you haven't yet visited. There are always shows taking place or events happening near you. Jot down those businesses in your notebook so you'll have a running list of the places you hope to explore. Although you might not be able to visit every single one of them, set aside a few hours here and there to check them out. These can be your partners tomorrow.

7. **Volunteer.** Seek out organizations that will feed your passion, or help a community you have a special connection with. Your voice and your time are the most important things you have. Don't let anyone take advantage in the name of the cause. Use your voice and time wisely— but use them!

It's easy to take your community for granted, so remind yourself that you reside in one of your favorite places in the world: home. Seek out the special attractions and discover new qualities you love about your area. Make it a point to know everything possible about where you live.

The process of learning about the place you call home will deepen your connections with your community and enrich your life beyond imagination. You'll come out with more knowledge, greater satisfaction, and undoubtedly a few new friendships, too!

* * *

At the time that I was doing all of this HIV education, I had an advanced knowledge about HIV and AIDS, but I wasn't totally aware of the impact that level of stress can have on a person, much less a family, community, or whole population of people. After Naomi's death, my mother was sad in a very quiet way. The bubbly mom I knew was not so any longer. I noticed something was wrong, and now I could see that my mother did her best to hide her crying. Yes, I knew HIV existed and that it was infecting many gay men who looked like me, and I knew it can cause health complications or even death, if ignored. But it was more of a distant thought, coupled with the blind acceptance that it would happen eventually anyway.

In a lifestyle like this—in an open relationship with my boyfriend, and with a career like mine—it was easy to become desensitized to how real the virus is. It was my will to deliver the message of awareness, action, safety, and self-worth, but I still lived a life full of contradictions. Those imperfections in the learning process are an ongoing part of evolving, both individually and professionally.

But it became more real to me when a friend whom I admired tested positive. He fell gravely ill, and much like my aunt years before, passed right before my eyes. I visited him in the hospital and saw with my own eyes the brutal effects of AIDS on the body. It was like reliving my aunt Naomi's suffering all over again. By the time he died, I realized how extremely lucky I was. I could have been infected many times over, and I had dodged the bullet that killed several people I loved.

I decided then and there that I didn't want to be that person. I didn't want my mother to have to visit me in the hospital and see a son she no longer recognized. I didn't want to become trapped in the frame of a withering body like my aunt Naomi, who could not speak or move. That was a full circle moment I knew I wanted to never complete. I wanted my story to be different—one filled with survival and happiness.

MY PAINFUL TURNING POINT

Delivering HIV results to a close friend in my chosen family was a significant turning point. He had been feeling sick for a while and suspected that he might have been infected, but he wouldn't get tested by anyone but me. So I filled out a sexual assessment, swabbed his cheek, and sent it to the Department of Health.

The normal protocol at that time was that it took two weeks to turn the results over to us. Every two weeks, I would get results by the stack, each result a possible life-changing event. It would either be nonreactive (negative) or reactive (positive), which would be an HIV-positive result.

Two weeks later, the dreaded news came in, and I was staring at a reactive result with my friend's name on it. I was afraid of how he was going to take the news, so I asked my supervisor if I could deliver the results after hours the next day, and he agreed.

That night I cried, feeling helpless and guilty. I had to reminded myself, "This is your job, Julio. Be honest with him. Be supportive and loving, and just remember that your job is to protect him. He will trust you as someone he knows he can count on."

The next day, I was nervous and sick, knowing I had to deliver this news after work. That evening, I closed the LGBTQIA+ center down and asked him to stay; his results were in. He agreed nervously. I sat him down in my office, and asked, "Are you ready to receive your results?" He said yes and I continued. "Mark, we have your results, and your test came back reactive to the HIV antibodies, which means you are HIV positive."

His initial reaction was a long stare and a light, "You must be joking," chuckle, in complete disbelief.

Delivering his results was one of the hardest things I have ever had to do, but I knew that receiving them was infinitely harder. I wanted to yell, "You're laughing? Really?" but I knew better. I knew that laughing is often a coping mechanism and a nervous tic for some people when faced with life-altering news like this.

Coupled with the sadness I felt for him, I was scared to death for myself because we had both engaged in some of the same risky behaviors. I partly blamed myself. It was my job to look out for him, and there I was, partying with him, going to the club with him, doing x, y, and z with him. Even though we were the same age, I felt like I had failed him, the person I should have been protecting, my best friend. This was when I finally became truly aware of my awesome responsibility, and how anything less than accepting and fulfilling it can result in devastation. It was a punch in the gut for me.

The responsibility to finally walk the talk had fallen on me. But I was torn. Maybe I didn't deserve to be spared. In fact, maybe I had HIV, too.

A BURIED VOICE LEADS TO SELFISH BEHAVIOR

When I was conducting HIV testing, which felt like twenty-four hours a day, part of me thought it was only a matter of time before I received the same HIV-positive results. I gave these results so often, with guys describing the very same sexual activity that I was involved in, that I felt like I would eventually come up positive, too. I had ignored the warnings that I was so often giving to others. These destructive thoughts grew and allowed me to compromise on everything I knew because I thought it was only a matter of time.

On a subconscious level, I accepted it. And because I accepted it, I engaged in even riskier sexual behavior, even though it was in direct contradiction to the work I was doing.

I wasn't advocating and asserting myself like I was coaching other people to do. I was not speaking up for myself in the way I was asking my community members to do. I was failing myself, and it felt like there was nothing I could do to stop.

A HARD LESSON TO LEARN ABOUT LOVE AND BOUNDARIES

On one dewy Sunday morning, after weeks of wrestling with the decision and countless discussions with Aaron, I felt an overwhelming sense of peace. I decided that a change from the city and partying was necessary, and a fresh start for us would be exactly what we needed. It would be a great way to refocus on our relationship and allow me to enter his world, which excited me. I was twenty-one years old and moving to Providence, Rhode Island, for a fresh start, away from the fast party life I had settled into in NYC. It was a move I believed was the only thing that could save my life from a dark ending if I continued down this path of indulgence and recklessness. It was also a decision that didn't come easy, but one that felt right at the time.

Providence was Aaron's hometown. So, in my eyes, this was a great way and the perfect time to become immersed into his world of family and friends. I was also excited about the prospects of a new move and learning more about his past. Even though I was overcome with excitement, dread snuck in at that very same moment.

I had to break the news to my mom and my five-year-old brother, David. My mom was going to be the hardest to tell. I had already left them once to find myself; now I had to tell my mom I was leaving her again and moving farther away to better myself. My twin brother, Angel, was doing time with no release date in sight, and I struggled at the thought of leaving her and little David alone.

While I worked up the courage to look my mom in the eye during lunch and tell her I was moving, it was little David who immediately burst into tears at the news, his face filling with pain and hurt because he understood even at five years old what was happening. His big brother, who had always provided a sense of safety, was leaving him. The look of disappointment and sadness in his eyes will be seared in my mind forever.

My mom wasn't happy, but hesitantly gave me her blessing. I handed in my resignation at work with no job secured in Providence, bought a car, emptied my savings, and rented a two-bedroom apartment, sight unseen, on the eastside of Providence on Colonial Road. I was leaving behind everything and everyone I knew.

A year into calling Providence home, however, that past of Aaron's I wanted to learn so much about finally caught up with me. Aaron began to stay out longer and longer on his nights out with his buddies, and twice did not return until the next morning. I was all about going out and having a good time and allowing my partner to do the same, but communication was always key. So, when we stopped talking mid-conversation, or his phone was turned off, I naturally grew suspicious. After doing some investigation, I learned he was messing around with an old high school friend who had come out after they graduated. This friend, I would later learn, was someone he'd always had a crush on.

At twenty-one years old, I wasn't emotionally tied to sex or monogamy. An open relationship agreement we had set up the year before made that easy for me. So the thought of him hooking up with someone didn't bother me as much as the thought of him laying up with someone he liked and not coming home until eight in the morning the next day, with no concern for my emotional well-being or the life that I had just given up to create something new for us.

That continued trespass of trust was a violation of the five years of effort he'd made to make me feel safe, and it spoke volumes to me. I could not tolerate or accept this lack of regard, not after everything I had done to sustain this relationship. So, at the sure price of further loneliness and isolation, after Aaron's *third* violation of not coming home, I ended the relationship and gave him a week to move out.

At this point, focusing on my career was in order. After the breakup, I began working at a social service homeless organization as a crisis intervention manager. I worked directly with the homeless community, including the mentally ill, those newly released from prison, disabled people, and chronic homeless populations in their most vulnerable and crisis-producing states. I was super excited to be back in the mix of working with the community in a whole new state, and with a whole new population. However, while in this role, I came to realize and appreciate that this would be the hardest job I would ever do, and that the effects of mental health and homelessness are real and dangerous if left untreated or unchecked.

I began to make friends at work and grow my social circle by going out and doing things outside of work with my coworkers, attempting to develop some sort of social life. Working at this new organization was great since my primary role was community engagement, and it allowed me to escape the office and be outside working in the community.

On a June summer morning, I was setting up my table at a community event. A man named Timothy was visiting all of the tables, introducing himself. He was a handsome twenty-four-year-old Puerto Rican guy with a brown buzz cut and hazel eyes.

We chatted for a bit, and he kept coming back to my table throughout the day. By the third visit, I figured he was interested in more than just the information on my table. He was there as a volunteer for a local soup kitchen and was seeking new work connections. By the end of the day, he asked me for my number, and we texted that night and set up a date for a few days later.

Friday rolled around and we met for lunch at a cafe where he told me more about himself. His mother died at a young age from cancer, and he was left by his dad with his slightly older sister, who put him in foster care in Massachusetts. Shortly after he was placed in foster care, his father passed away from diabetes. He said that he knew any chance of leaving the foster care system disappeared with his dad's death, and he aged out of foster care at eighteen.

As it turned out, he was new to Providence and didn't know anyone.

I instantly felt compassion for him.

Before we knew it, we were seeing each other every other day after work, and he began staying over three or four nights a week. Every moment we were together, we had a great time. It was especially great because after a long day of working with people who consistently needed help, I needed a break and someone to talk to beyond friendly small talk. While many homeless individuals are so kind and appreciative of the work we do, some homeless people yelled and cursed, or left their emotional baggage or other foreign substances on us.

A month into us talking, Timothy called me at work one afternoon to tell me he'd lost his job, and asked if he could stay with me for a week. He was already staying with me most nights anyway, so I said yes. I wanted companionship. And I reasoned that I was by myself, working exhausting days, and he was looking for a place to live. I could definitely use the money, too, and assumed that he'd start paying me a portion of the rent as soon as he moved in. To me, it was a win-win, so I crossed a lot of my own boundaries and broke all my own rules when I said yes. Needless to say, those are not the right reasons to get into a relationship or allow someone to move in with you.

Things seemed great at first, and I was happy to have someone to spend time with, but I soon started noticing things that really bothered me. Timothy's energy decreased, and his mood was quick to change. He could go from happy to upset and accusatory in a span of minutes. I'd asked him many times if he'd found another job or even looked for one, but he never followed through. He smoked cigarettes and weed all day, every day, evident by the full ashtrays I cleaned when I came home from work. His behavior turned erratic and unstable, he acted jealous, and our relationship became extremely co-dependent.

Two months after he moved in, he finally disclosed that he was bipolar but wasn't taking his medication. Toward the end of our relationship, I found out that Timothy also had schizophrenic disorder. But by that point, I felt stuck and didn't know what to do. Then, to freak me out even further, he started saying that my place was haunted, that he heard things rattling around in other rooms or felt something touch him. This really scared me and made me uncomfortable on so many levels because I suddenly realized his reality was becoming more altered for him, day by day. I knew this situation needed to change. But how?

WHEN EMPATHY IGNORES RISK

I felt increasingly alone in Rhode Island. None of my family knew that I was in this situation and that I felt trapped. How could I ask him to leave? He had nowhere to go, no family and no resources, and I worked in the only homeless shelter in the area!

After several weeks of mustering up the courage, I took my lunch break and headed home to tell Timothy it was not going to work and that I needed him to move out. I offered help with anything he might need, but he didn't even look at me. He didn't exactly look happy, and gave me no other response but a smirk, as if he knew this talk was coming. I'm glad I did it during lunch, as it gave me the day to go back to work and allow things to cool down if they got heated again. That had become our routine. But little did I know this time around that a cooling-down period wasn't going to happen.

A few nights later, after a long, tiring week at work, I accepted an invitation out to Platforms, a local gay club, with friends. I came home from work, excited because it was Friday and I didn't have to work tomorrow. I was still not sure if it would be cool with Timothy. I walked in the door while talking to my boy, Speedy, on my cell phone.

"Hey, hunnyyyyy," Speedy said. "What are you wearing tonight? I'm ready to get fuckeddd up and hear the new Missy! And you need to get out the house so don't say no!"

"Boyyy, I don't know?! I really don't want to go anywhere. We been arguing, and I just don't trust what this kid would do here or when I get back. He already said last week he would show up at Platform if he had to."

"He ain't going to do shit. He's definitely not coming to no Platform because he would be dragged out of there, which you already know. Besides, ya not together so I wouldn't let him control you. This is the third weekend you ain't go nowhere. That's crazy!" He was right and we both knew it: I needed a break. But I was still hesitant.

"I don't know, I'm going to be thinking about him showing up all night."

"Trust me, he not going to try nothing at the club," Speedy said.

"Ugh bitch, okay. You lucky you're my brother. And I love you! Let me shower and get ready." I was finally getting excited about going out!

"Be there soon," Speedy said, and we hung up.

Timothy, who was always jealous of Speedy and our closeness, most likely heard the details of the conversation, as he sat looking out the window chain smoking his cigarettes.

That night, everything changed. I felt like I was walking on eggshells as I gathered my outfit for the night. I began to take a shower when suddenly, Timothy charged into the bathroom through what I thought was a locked door, wielding a kitchen knife. With just one look at his face, I knew he was in a whole other state of mind and being. The way he looked right through me terrified me. He screamed, "You are not going anywhere!"

I attempted to run out of the shower, soaking wet and totally naked. I struggled to grip the shower wall and shower curtain, anything I could find, attempting to not lose my balance. The dry floor mat allowed my foot to grip the floor and propel myself out the bathtub and out the bathroom door.

But when I pushed him to get away, he fell and hit his forehead on the door latch, and it split a three-inch gash across his forehead. And, since head wounds notoriously bleed a lot, it was like a faucet turned on. The sight of his own blood panicked Timothy to tears for a moment and then enraged him even more. Both the sight and amount of his blood on the flat white walls terrified me. Timothy chased me into the living room and jumped on me, wrestling me down to the ground.

With blood pouring down his face onto mine, he put his knees on my shoulders to hold me down, then held the kitchen knife to my throat. I was at his mercy. I could feel the serrated edges of the knife on my skin and I silently prayed he wouldn't kill me. He told me that I would never leave him and that I was not going anywhere.

Then, staring down at me. He reached over to the coffee table, took the half-smoked cigarette, and lit it, the knife still in hand. He smirked and then removed the bright orange lit cigarette from his lips and seared my wet skin into a perfectly burned circle on my face, below my right eye.

"Now, where are you going?" he asked, staring down at me with a sinister look. It was one of the most humiliating, degrading, and surreal things to ever happen to me. I started to silently sob, afraid to utter a single response, afraid that my agony was fueling this monster.

I was terrified. Looking into his eyes and seeing a void of

emotion, I began repeating his name, trying to get him to snap out of that trance, but he didn't respond. After a few moments, I stopped crying. I'd resigned myself to whatever was about to happen. Thankfully, this silence somehow seemed to startle him. Suddenly, as quickly as his violent behavior had started, he snapped out of it.

As soon as I saw the void leave his eyes, I knew his trance was breaking, and with his weight lightening, I pushed him off me. In those moments, with the sound coming back to my ears, a banging on the window was getting louder and louder. Outside, Speedy and a few other friends were banging on the window, yelling at Timothy and yelling for me. They had seen everything and were both furious and terrified at what had been done to me.

Timothy looked at the window, dropped the knife, and ran into the bathroom. I quickly kicked the knife under the sofa so he could not find it if he came out again. Then I opened my bedroom window on the ground level to let my friends in, and they helped me quickly pack my bags so I could leave.

I survived that night, and I ended the relationship. Still, I would carry the scars for life, both mentally and physically. Seeing that burn in the mirror every time I looked at my face was a reminder of that incident, like I somehow deserved it, or like I'd opened the door for the abuse.

What disturbed me most was that I had ignored all of Timothy's warning signs and proceeded with the relationship. This made me question whether I had healed from all of my past traumas. Had I made my decisions based on my own need for love and approval, or on what I believed was right for me? I didn't have a support system at that time, outside of my small group of friends, and I certainly wasn't strong enough to advocate for myself. Or so I thought.

A few months after that incident, I had a series of skin treatments and chemical peels to reduce the visibility of the scar. But

I will never be able to erase that memory. That event when I was twenty-three years old was one of the big turning points in my life.

That whole experience with Timothy taught me just how real mental health issues are, and even more so how harmful they can become if left unaddressed. It taught me that medication compliance can be the difference between life and death for someone in his position, and mine. It also taught me that, in the future, I could be empathetic and try to help someone without putting myself at risk. It taught me to not ignore the red flags and to not ignore that inner voice that tells you when you are not safe.

While it was certainly a horrific event in my life, it was also a lesson I needed to learn. I had broken so many of my own rules because of my empathy for someone, and also my need to be needed, that it almost got me killed.

I look back at all of the risky situations I put myself in and know, without a shadow of a doubt, that I could have benefited immensely from a safe space that provided support and access to someone like me.

A SURPRISE STICK

After ending the abusive relationship with Timothy, I decided a break from relationships was in order. Dates were a no-go. I denied "special friend" requests. Anything that looked like it could go down a relationship path, I avoided or sabotaged. The only interactions I permitted myself would be a one- or two-night stand and the occasional club hook-up.

However, that got old quick, and I started dating a new guy a year later. Eddie was an HIV counselor and tester, which I thought was cool because of my background. After a few months of dating and endless protected sex, we both wanted to stop condom use altogether after a few slip-ups. Of course, those slip-ups helped us determine that we loved it! And we wanted to keep having unprotected sex.

I had not been tested for two years at this point, and he wanted me to get tested for HIV, given my year of flings. His approach was off to say the least, and probably illegal. I didn't see it coming. When I went to pick him up one day at his office, I'd barely walked through the door when he said, "Come here, let me see a finger." I knew what he wanted to do then, and why he had invented this ill-prepared setup of needing a ride.

He didn't even ask me if I wanted to get tested! But I knew I couldn't refuse, as that would be sounding the bullhorn that I had something to hide or had done something reckless, knowingly putting him at risk. I liked Eddie, but I did not expect to get a surprise HIV test, which was off-putting. It felt like a setup. But I understood why.

I surrendered my index finger, he stuck it and drew blood, then tapped the blood droplets on a light-blue HIV rapid results testing pad. Then he asked, "Is there anything I should be scared about?"

"Really? *Now* you want to have that conversation?" I blurted. He chuckled and fixed his eyes once again on the mystery result window that sat between us. I lied and said, "No, of course not," hoping the falsehood of my blatant lie was not evident, as I was trying to keep my composure.

I added, "But make sure you do yours, too." His eyes widened in surprise. I picked up the all-too-familiar remaining test kit, opened it, and took his finger, making sure I got a huge droplet for his test.

And then I just sat there, petrified, all the while thinking of the slip-ups in the year past and the random hook-ups. *Maybe I am positive*, I thought. *Maybe I've even infected him.* These thoughts ran in loops.

When you believe you are already HIV-positive, you lose hope. That thought creates a domino effect of compromise that can create immense damage. From that point forward, you live in fear. You don't see past a certain point because you don't know if you'll really live to see past that certain point.

HIV tests have improved big time since the days of cheek swabs and a two-week wait for results. Now, it only takes twenty minutes! No going home to wait it out, no preparing yourself to learn the results in two weeks, and no ghosting or not coming back.

We sat in Eddie's office talking, waiting. I was trying to keep the conversation coherent, but my mind was figuring out which strategy to employ if my results came back positive. *What am I going to say? How am I going to act? Am I going to act surprised?*

I decided I'd act surprised. Obviously, I had been with people before him and he before me. And we hadn't gotten tested before jumping into the bliss of unprotected sex.

Twenty minutes later, the testing buzzer sounded, cutting into our conversation. Results were ready. As he went to retrieve them, I studied his walk, both to the other side of the room and back, and looked for any signs of distress on his face or change in his gait. I got nothing. He stared at the result for a few seconds, then looked up and said, "You are all set. It's negative." I could tell he was relieved. God knows I was. And if the faint line coming through for him stayed the same, he was negative, too.

Just like that, a year of fear was over in twenty minutes. The worry and the stress, resigning myself to a life of living with HIV, all of it was for nothing.

HIV doesn't have a face. We've all heard that before. It doesn't select people based on their gender or race or sexual preference. It doesn't care about how much you love your partner or how much your partner loves you. It is an opportunistic infection, so all it needs is one opening. I have seen everybody get it: poor, rich, Black, white, woman, man, pregnant, senior citizen, seventeen years old, fifteen years old, and thirteen years old. It does not discriminate. It does not respect anyone.

But there, in the office, I was given a second chance at living a life free of HIV. Now that I knew I was negative, I felt a strong responsibility to make different decisions. I had to own up to taking responsibility for all of the fucked-up shit I was doing while I was out in the community preaching the direct opposite. And with time, I started the journey of changing my behavior, day by day, experience by experience.

Now I get tested regularly, every six months, even if I am not putting myself at risk, just for that peace of mind. I'll admit, the anxiety while you are waiting for that test never goes away. The peace of mind of knowing your status, I promise, will outweigh the fear of not knowing.

BEING CALLED HOME

The call was one I dreaded. Grandma Virginia had always been the head of our family, the center in which the whole family met for holidays and weekends. And now Mom was explaining that she was just diagnosed with stage 4 cancer, and it was only a matter of weeks before she would no longer be with us. *A couple of weeks?* It was two days before I was back in Newark at my grandmother's house, at her bedside on Mt Prospect and 2nd Ave. It was in my visits to her in her final days, reliving my childhood car drives and Avon trips with her, that an overwhelming sense of peace flooded me. And I knew home was where I belonged and where I needed to continue to do my work creating safe spaces and working with LGBTQIA+ allies and advocates in communities of color. Up to this point, I honestly struggled with the decision.

At twenty-eight, after making some incredible friends who became family, some great experiences, and meeting the love of my life Rafael, it was a move I was ready for and we were welcoming. Providence was a learning experience in being an adult and taking responsibility for myself, and it was the first time I lived and felt completely on my own. This was essential in me learning how to set priorities for what I wanted out of life and where I wanted to end up. I call it my bridge period from adolescence to full adulthood. It was the point where I had to make a choice—a conscious choice to take what I had learned, apply it, and strive to live it every day, not just in my professional life where all could see, but also in my personal life where it needed to be most reflective.

CHAPTER 5

Safe Spaces, Past and Present

"As people of color, we have a potent power—and a responsibility
—to change events around us, not just professionally,
but spiritually and politically as well."

—MICHELLE HERRERA MULLIGAN, WRITER AND EDITOR

All throughout history, and still today, LGBTQIA+ bars and other gay-affirming social gatherings have been a lifeline of support for the LGBTQIA+ community. In the early days, the bars were not only a place where gay and lesbian people could gather in an establishment that felt inclusive and somewhat safe, but they were also the breeding grounds upon which the gay rights movement was organized and started.

The particular story that most people are familiar with is the 1969 Stonewall Riots, which was three nights of coordinated LGBTQIA+ rebellion against police raids at the Stonewall Inn on Christopher Street.[4] It was definitely *not* the first time gay people had risen up against the constant barrage of threats from police, but it was consciously labelled by the LGBTQIA+ community as the first in order to globally commemorate the movement that had been bubbling underneath the surface for years, and which

4 "Stonewall Riots: The Beginning of the LGBT Movement," CivilRights.org, July 22, 2019, https://civilrights. org/2009/06/22/stonewall-riots-the-beginning-of-the-lgbt-movement/.

finally triggered activist movements in many other countries as well. The word "safe" implies a certain comfort level internally, but it demands a rock-hard exterior to protect the treasure inside. After all, the right to exist and prosper is the most basic human right.

Even as HIV was becoming more prevalent in the eighties within the gay community, there were no safe spaces for us. No LGBTQIA+ centers, and none of the world-renowned organizations we so appreciate today.

The lack of safe spaces made it both logistically and psychologically difficult for an HIV-positive gay man to get treated. In order for him to get medication to treat the disease, he needed to be able to talk to someone to find the appropriate care. In addition, he needed to have a safe environment that allowed them to speak freely and frankly regarding his sexual experiences, which, during that time, were frequently met with suspicion and fear.

In an attempt to fill that need, many private homes of LGBTQIA+ people became a safe space, while some churches and the formation of the ballroom house scenes provided some relief to the HIV/AIDS infections that were ravaging the gay community. The activists at that time represented a safe space themselves and went on to lead and create organizations and safe spaces we hold up as models today. Some of these heroes and pioneers include Marsha P. Johnson, Sylvia Rivera, Dennis deLeon, John Giorno, Moises Agosto, Barbara Lee, and Phil Wilson.

The heroes, sheroes, and pioneers I listed above hold special places in the LGBTQIA+ community because of what they believed, and how they took what they believed and made it tangible. They became examples for a community in need of something they could touch and see. These were leaders who represented and fought for safe spaces, creators in their own right. These names represent a fraction of the activists that have shaped the LGBTQIA+ community and where we are today. This book is filled with their contributions. Please take the time to learn about these leaders and others. Enrich yourself with what they stood for, learn from their lessons, and be inspired.

LEARNING THE HISTORY TO BE A BETTER ADVOCATE

One way I became an effective advocate was to educate myself on the history of the community I desired to serve. You must know your own history to truly appreciate it, preserve it, and move forward in the direction of progress. But you must also know this of the community members you wish to work with so they may progress, as well.

For me, this includes Newark's LGBTQIA+ history and the lessons others have learned along the way through different experiences, both positive and negative. Newark is sometimes overlooked and remains in the shadow of New York City in general, but the truth is that Newark has an extraordinarily rich history that deserves a spotlight.

At a time when media and social media are flooding our minds with the latest and greatest fashion, gadgets, gossip and bad news, good news, and everything in between, it's important we continue to tell the stories our gay predecessors have preserved and fought for. We also have to share the tales told and lived by our grandmothers, grandfathers, aunts, uncles, and other loved ones. There are thousands of untold stories, and each story is relevant, like necessary pieces to a beautifully complete puzzle. We must remember to honor our history and follow their lead.

In honoring my history, I choose to focus mainly on creating safe spaces and designing programming for at-risk communities. I work primarily with Black and Latinx LGBTQIA+ communities. The reason for that, of course, is that it's personal to me. I'm a Latino gay man, disproportionately at a higher risk for just about everything that can negatively impact or end my life, especially as it pertains to HIV, because of the lack of health literacy and access and the social economic status of Black and Brown communities.[5]

Timothy Stewart-Winter and Whitney Strub share wisdom about the AIDS crisis and the historical response in Newark:

From the start, the AIDS epidemic disproportionately affected poor communities and people of color, both heavily represented in Newark. By 1989, the city ranked fifth in the nation in total number of AIDS cases. While the epidemic's devastation affected men, women, and children of all sexualities, gay men of color found themselves without access to many of the social institutions, such as church and family, that heterosexuals often took for granted. The ballroom scene provided crucial emotional sustenance, community, and support during the 1980s and 90s. Anthropologist Karen McCarthy Brown, who studied the Houses of Newark during the 1990s, described voguing as a form of ritualized "performative anger," as when 30-year-old Angel Vizcaya unleashed several white doves from a skirt while walking a runway in 1998—a powerful performance delivered a week after his brother had died from AIDS-related complications. She also noted that in the ballroom scene, Latinos (the fastest growing local demographic) "count as blacks".

...Meanwhile, grassroots activists strained to fill the growing gaps in service provision brought about by the loss of manufacturing jobs, the Reagan administration's budget cuts to cities and social services, and the growing number of uninsured Americans concentrated in urban

5   White gay men, on average, get infected with HIV at a 1:22 rate. The ratio for Latino gay men is 1:3 and Black gay men is 1:2. In case you don't know what this means, it means that one in twenty-two white gay men will be infected with HIV in their lifetime, in comparison to one in three Latino men and one in two Black men. This is just one example of the wide disparity in this community. Poverty and lack of education are also barriers that are known to affect access to quality healthcare, HIV awareness education, and primary care prevention services. (Source: https://www.cdc.gov/hiv/group/racialethnic/index.html)

areas. The Newark Community Project for People with AIDS was incorporated in 1988, and other important organizations followed. ASPIRA, a long-running Latino youth group, began to sponsor HIV/AIDS prevention education workshops, and in 2000, Gary Paul Wright founded the Office of African American Gay Concerns, a community organization with a focus on HIV/AIDS prevention work.[6]

We know that in the late eighties in Newark, we were fifth in the country in terms of HIV infection rates. We also knew it clearly affected poor people and people of color, which constituted the majority of Newark. Gay men especially found no places to turn to, except for the Newark Ballroom Houses that provided safe spaces in the midst of the epidemic. It was in this space that drag performances took place and flourished.

The houses provided safe spaces and empowered house members to release not only their anger rooted in abandonment, fear, and survival but also their gifts of creativity, individuality, and uniqueness on the dance floor, in a place where it would be welcomed, safe, and celebrated. This provided a release of acceptance and a high like no other. It was also in these houses where the message of safer sex, accessing treatment, and surviving on the streets was delivered.

Young gay Black and Latino men are still dying at higher rates. But, from my own experience (and near misses), they don't have to suffer this fate. If they had a safe space and some level of support, they could bypass a lot of these tragic experiences by connecting to a wider community of advocates with shared experiences. Fortunately, we can look to history for early successful examples.

---

6   Timothy Stewart Winter and Whitney Strub, "Queer Newark by Timothy Stewart-Winter and Whitney Strub: AIDS Crisis and Response," OutHistory.org, https://outhistory.org/exhibits/show/queer-newark/crisis-and-response.

THE VOGUE BALLROOM SCENE

The Vogue Ballroom scene was a young African American and Latinx underground culture that first started in Harlem, where LGBTQIA+ youth and young adults competed for trophies and money—or sometimes just glory.

The Vogue Ballroom community in America has played a vital role in the success of supporting countless local LGBTQIA+ centers, safe spaces, and some of our most at-risk Black and Latinx LGBTQIA+ youth. Many times, these ballroom houses offered refuge to youth and adults in the community who had been kicked out or disowned by their families and had no other place to live. The ballroom houses became their homes, and the residents their chosen family.

These balls, and kiki sessions for our newbies in training, have been used in the past and still today to raise funds for houses to support their members and also to legitimize the official presence of a center where LGBTQIA+ people can seek refuge or simply have a space to be their true selves. In case you're unfamiliar with kiki sessions or the kiki scene, it's for new, younger folks, even elementary-school-aged people, to train and practice their moves before they enter the competitive ballroom scene. They're often called boot camps, and they have competitions so the attendees can practice against each other and build their reputations. No one goes into the ballroom scene (the older and more experienced Voguers) without having practiced in kiki sessions.

As Mark Lindores so beautifully explains in his article about the beginnings of voguing:

> Though it rose to prominence in the mid-1980s, New York's drag ball culture can be traced right back to the first Annual Odd Fellows Ball (later known as the Faggots Ball or Fairies Ball), held at Harlem's Hamilton Lodge No.710 in 1867, where men and women gathered to dress

in drag to compete as the most convincing impersonator of the opposite sex. The balls steadily gathered momentum throughout the jazz age and early 20th century, before rising racial tensions, both in ball culture and America as a whole, erupted in the 1960s when Crystal LaBeija accused organizers of racism and rigging the vote, costing her the first prize in the All-American Camp Beauty Contest. It prompted her to begin holding her own black ballroom events, where attendees were later welcomed into "houses" and asked to compete in a variety of categories, including Butch Queen Realness, European Runway, Town & Country, Face, and Executive.

Offering a home to those that don't have one, each "house" had a "Mother" or a "Father" who took on a mentoring role and looked after young, mostly Black or Latino gay men, known as "children," who had found themselves the victims of rejection by their biological families, as well as often suffering abuse, homelessness and addiction. The Mothers and Fathers of the houses became surrogates, often providing people with a home and a place where they belonged while they competed against the other houses, a host of which followed in quick succession—including the House of Xtravaganza, the House of Omni and the House of Ninja, among many others.

As many of the children's lives had been marred by violence, rejection and hostility, the battle element was introduced as a non-violent way to achieve supremacy. As the sentiment and loyalty of the houses echoed gang culture of the 1940s and 1950s, the battles were part dance-off, part fashion face-off. Though the winner only received a trophy, the real prize was the sense of achievement and acceptance that came from it. As Dorian Corey, Mother of the House of Corey, says in *Paris Is Burning*, "In Ballroom we can be whatever we want. It is our Oscars—our chance to be a superstar."

As competition between the houses intensified, voguing emerged as the trademark dance style of the drag balls. "It all started at an after-hours club called Footsteps on 2nd Avenue and 14th Street," says DJ David DePino, a legend of the scene thanks to his sets at clubs such as Paradise Garage and Tracks. "Paris Dupree was there, and a bunch of black queens were throwing shade at each other. Paris had a Vogue magazine in her bag, and while she was dancing, she took it out, opened it up to a page where a model was posing and then stopped in that pose on the beat. Then she turned to the next page and stopped in the new pose, again on the beat. Then another queen came up and did another pose in front of Paris, and then Paris went in front of her and did another pose. This was all shade—they were all trying to make a prettier pose than each other—and it soon caught on at the balls. At first, they called it posing and then, because it started from *Vogue* magazine, they called it voguing."

As new dancers brought their own ideas and identities into the scene, the dance evolved from Old Way (almost static, balletic poses transitioning from one to another) to New Way (based on the traditional voguing but incorporating more athleticism and martial arts-inspired moves, and best exemplified by Willi Ninja, and, later Vogue Fem (ultra-feminine choreography with intricate posturing, hair whips and deathdrops), so too did the music. With attitude and arrogance key characteristics of voguing, the music evolved from classic disco and Philly soul to pounding house beats, sliced up with snatches of dialogue and film monologues.[7]

---

7   Mark Lindores, "Voguing: A Brief History of the Ballroom," *Mixmag*, October 10, 2018, https://mixmag.net/feature/a-brief-history-of-voguing.

Ball houses will always continue to act as safe spaces. The purpose of family and belonging is universal, and these safe spaces will continue speaking to the hearts of a community that is often outcast and feels pushed to the edges of society. Many are dumped from their families, and others are kicked out of their homes. Knowing about the role of ball houses in LGBTQIA+ history allows us to honor and appreciate the efforts made long before we entered the scene.

In May of 1989, the singer Madonna entered a Village club and was introduced to a few members of the LGBTQIA+ community at an event in New York called the Love Ball, and she fell in love with the music and the scene. She asked a few of the dancers to teach her how to vogue and ended up hiring several of them to participate in her new music video for *Vogue*, which propelled the ballroom scene into the mainstream world. This led to the filming of *Truth and Dare*, an exposé and look at her life behind the scenes as she toured internationally with many of them. The film does not give you an in-depth look at ballroom houses, but does document very well the rise of ballroom into mainstream pop culture.[8]

BALLS AS SAFE SPACES

As glamorous as that bit of history is, as a Black or Brown LGBTQIA+ advocate, it is important to know that the ballroom scene is rooted in rebellion. It began in the late nineteenth century, when LGBTQIA+ communities organized balls, or drags, to show their opposition to laws banning people from crossdressing. Harlem was first. And the second city to start a ballroom scene was none other than Newark, New Jersey. City number three was Philadelphia. Today, because of *Paris Is Burning*, Madonna's

8 Lindores, "Voguing."

"Vogue," and FX's *Pose*, legendary balls are still an integral part of the LGBTQIA+ community, and the ballroom dance culture has become a harbor of safety for many globally. Countless LGBTQIA+ safe spaces or young organizations depend on balls for the support and consistent connecting of new young people needing support opportunities and a safe space.[9]

My first experience of the ballroom scene was in my early days of visiting the Village and attending one for myself at the famous Stonewall Inn. Much like the beats of the church I had experienced earlier in my youth, this was a new beat and a new church.

This scene has been vital for enriching my personal experience, as I learned from many of the LGBTQIA+ teenagers who came in to release a power within them. It was my first contact with a boldness I had never witnessed—a boldness I longed for. These same teens would later become the house moms and dads, the DJs, the promoters, and also the teachers, bankers, and gatekeepers of the community.

Now, it's one thing—an amazing thing—to know all about this and have the seed of an idea. But, if you're just starting, how do you actually go about creating a safe space in your community?

UNDERSTANDING THE "WHY" IS THE FIRST STEP TO CREATING A SAFE SPACE

For decades, discrimination and bullying have imposed on the rights of the LGBTQIA+ community to gather in a safe space. As a Brown gay man who has endured his fair share of both, it is my mission to help create amazing safe spaces for LBGTQIA+ young people and adults alike to be and express their authentic self. I also want others to connect to healthy social networks and development opportunities to keep them out of harm's way and,

9   Lindores, "Voguing."

as the title indicates, to keep them *safe*. The freedom to speak and act without fear of intimidation or violence promotes strength and confidence, qualities that are needed in the LGBTQIA+ community.

There is a movement in the LGBTQIA+ community to create a culture of safety in all aspects of life in the world, not just our community. Now more than ever, having a safe space in your workplace, school, or organization is so important because it allows a culture of inclusion and diversity to exist across each of the places you spend time in. Because we all spend so much time at work, the line between our domestic life and our work life can get blurrier and blurrier as the years go on. The right to exist freely in the workplace and community should not be blurred.

But why the need for a safe space at work, school, or your organization? So that we are more than just tolerated—so that we are accepted without fear of harm. Safe spaces promote understanding. They welcome participation. They encourage authenticity, vulnerability, connection, and transparency, all of which have been shown to increase engagement and morale at work and in a community and, therefore, increase productivity and drive—all powers that we possess.

I found that working in the Project WOW LGBTQIA+ center really helped me see life through the lens of other people who look like me and who understand what being in church and being gay means. I was surrounded by other young gay men, both clients and team members. I heard their stories and learned from their struggles as I struggled. They opened up about their failures, shared secrets, and also celebrated what was great about life. I felt unjudged, free, and seen. The safe space of this role ensured I had the support and people around me to lean on, or to check me if I acted reckless or was heading into trouble. After all, it was this space that empowered me to come out to my mom.

In contrast, without a safe space, I found myself literally fighting for my life alone in another state, isolated without the structure and support that often comes from family. Trapped without structure.

THE NEEDS ASSESSMENT: CREATING SPACES PEOPLE WANT AND NEED

When we design a safe space, first, we must make clear the need or goal. Then, we assess the resources available, assemble the team, identify the space, ensure community buy-in and training, and identify the necessary resources.

Many LGBTQIA+ safe spaces begin with social gatherings and support groups, support groups for parents, and workshops. Many times, these groups or gatherings are already happening in your community, like at colleges and nonprofit organizations. It can be a bit scary, but don't be afraid to reach out and ask for help, a tour, or a meeting to utilize the wealth of experience and support they can provide.

One of the very first steps in creating an LGBTQIA+ safe space is to gather information that will provide you with a comprehensive understanding of the community and the experiences of the LGBTQIA+ people who live or work there. It will also be helpful to know how the community has responded to LGBTQIA+ safe spaces in the past, what ideas have been tried, and what's been found to work and what doesn't. All of these things are an important part of a getting to know your community. A great way to gather this information is performing a proper Community Needs Assessment, which is a method of learning about your community's needs and wants.

When it comes to a community as a whole and the individuals who live in it, you'll want the information you gather to be focused on these areas: knowledge, attitudes, and beliefs.

1. Measure their **knowledge** around what it is you are trying to create. What do they know or wish to learn about safe spaces? Allow them to share and listen.

2. Next, feel out their **attitudes** around the idea and concept of safe spaces and why they need to exist. Have they worked in the past? If so, why? If not, why not?

3. Assess the innate **beliefs** that LGBTQIA+ people have about what you are trying to create. Why are their beliefs shaped this way? What about those beliefs feel true to them?

When creating a focus group or organizing a meeting for the first time to get to know the community, the answers around any of these questions will reveal three key things:

- Psychological or logistical limitations and barriers

- Misinformation and stigmas you may need to address

- Your safe space top priorities

The goal is to first become informed about what the community needs and is requesting. Next, you want to build a dialogue and create an easy way for the community member to take part in the conversation. Finessing the right balance of hearing out the community while also aiming to fulfill your goals and objectives—*this* is where the real magic in organizing starts. With experience, you get better at the balancing act.

Before gathering the community, you should check in with some of the LGBTQIA+ community leaders, popular opinion leaders, or gatekeepers to ask them when the best time is to approach their community for conversation. Who should be invited, who absolutely needs to be prioritized, and what are the best places for the meeting to take place?

Now, you might ask, why are these questions so important? Your gatekeepers, as I like to call them, are persons who often know the language, lingo, and culture of the local LGBTQIA+ community. This person already has the community reputation, so their word is trusted, and they are considered a reliable entity. If you partner with them, you have just partnered with areas of the community that may be the hardest to reach or groups that you didn't even know existed.

They should be able to identify other LGBTQIA+ people in the community who would be a good fit for the process. It may even be someone who has a natural ability to lead whose skills and ability need nurturing or mentoring.

You'll want to ask who they think should be invited, what barriers might affect people from showing up, and how long the meeting should be. You need to decide whether food, bus tickets, or other incentives should be available. The goal here is to make sure you are meeting the community where they are.

I find many LGBTQIA+ people are willing to participate and help because they're aware of the lack of safe spaces they couldn't find growing up, whether in school, work, or the community. Many of them were bullied or experienced rejection, so they're ready and willing to be allies to the younger and older versions of themselves.

It is important that whoever leads this effort as a facilitator or planner is personable and outgoing, but also trained and skilled in the interview process. They must be empathic and kind, but also focused and clear.

This part of the process is meant for not only collecting information for yourself but also making sure the community and its leaders know that each of their voices matter and that the information we're seeking needs to come straight from them. This can be utilized as a way for the community members to take ownership and feel included in the process.

The Community Needs Assessment is crucial because you want to build trust and fair representation of the community you are going to serve, and you want to be as informed as possible. This is the first step in using a peer-led and peer-driven approach to creating the space. Ultimately, it'll help you envision what the space is going to look like, what its voice in the community will sound like, and what it represents.

To create an LGBTQIA+ safe space, the most important piece of the Community Needs Assessment is to make sure that the people who are at the table are going to be the people you are going to serve and serve with, no matter what those voices look like, and no matter how hard the input might be to hear sometimes. It is important that they are not token members, but that their opinions are valued and turned into action.

You do not want your core group to look all the same, unless that is the specific LGBTQIA+ group within the community you are trying to engage. The more diverse you can make your advisory or core group, the better it will be for everyone. This may also mean breaking up the focus groups into smaller groups for more personal talks regarding each segment's needs. For instance, you might create a trans advisory group or Latin issues advisory group.

In sum, instead of trying to sell your idea, utilize a Community Needs Assessment so the safe space becomes an invested goal and vision for all. Here's one to get you started.

COMMUNITY NEEDS ASSESSMENT QUESTIONNAIRE

This Community Needs Assessment[10] is designed to help us understand gaps in service and community needs. Remember that a community assessment helps you get a comprehensive understanding of the LGBTQIA+ community in a relatively simple and fast way. It should not be confused with a needs assessment, which is usually a much more in-depth, lengthy, and involved task.

The following is a recreation of a Community Needs Assessment that you can utilize and modify with your own questions so you can learn more about the community safe space's needs. Just make sure you know what information you want to collect and why.

* * *

Please fill all sections to the best of your ability. Information is kept confidential. We value your input. Thank you for taking the time to help us make this community a happier, healthier place to live.

10   "New Zealand: International Affairs Discussion Document Launch." MENA Report, Albawaba (London) Ltd., May 2019.

Demographic Information

Occupation

Community Role

Town

County

Age
- ☐ Under 18
- ☐ 18–24
- ☐ 25–34
- ☐ 35–44
- ☐ 45–54
- ☐ 55–64
- ☐ 65–74
- ☐ 75+

Gender Identity

Race

Ethnicity

Education Level
- ☐ Grades 0–8
- ☐ Grades 9–12 (non-graduate)
- ☐ High school graduate
- ☐ Associate degree
- ☐ Bachelor's degree
- ☐ Master's or doctor's degree

Military Status
- ☐ Veteran
- ☐ Active
- ☐ N/A

For each category below, identify the three most important needs. Place the numbers one to three in the "#" column beside the needs you find most important. Please place a "1" next to the most important need, "2" next to the second most important need, and "3" next to the third most important need. Select only three needs per category. Please take the time to consider each category carefully.

Housing

_____ More monthly rental assistance programs

_____ Increased availability of security/utility deposit programs

_____ More counseling resources for homeowners

_____ Grants to make homeownership more affordable

_____ Programs to provide free home repair

_____ More income-based rental housing for disabled individuals and seniors

_____ More community support for homeless families

_____ More community support for homeless veterans

_____ Other:

Health

_____ More community focus on preventative healthcare

_____ Provide more education on maintaining personal hygiene

_____ More payment assistance programs for adult dental and/or hearing services

_____ More vision assistance programs for adults

_____ Increasing the community awareness of available health resources

_____ Early childhood nutrition education

_____ Emphasis on reinforcing healthy eating habits in schools

_____ Affordable nutritional counseling

_____ More awareness of available food resources

_____ More assistance and resources for victims of domestic violence

_____ Other:

Employment

_____ More jobs with better pay and benefits

_____ More training for the types of jobs available in the area

_____ Affordable transportation to and from jobs

_____ Affordable childcare during work hours

_____ Increasing community's knowledge of employment resources

_____ Improving workforce readiness skills of individuals entering the workforce

_____ Other:

Income and Asset Building

_____ Anonymous and confidential budget counseling

_____ More education on how to build assets

_____ Information on how to access free credit counseling

_____ Anonymous and confidential savings counseling

_____ More information on how to access financial resources

_____ Increasing the community's knowledge of available mainstream financial resources

_____ Other:

Civic Engagement

_____ Increasing the community's skills and knowledge for leadership development

_____ More citizenship classes

_____ More education on how to join neighborhood associations, community boards, advisory groups, or similar organizations

_____ Increased awareness of civic activities

_____ Other:

Support Services

_____ Child support

_____ Legal services

_____ Youth services

_____ Meal programs

_____ Life skills programs

_____ Substance abuse services

_____ Emotional abuse services

_____ Physical abuse services

_____ Transportation services

_____ Other:

Which of the following areas do you believe requires the most funding and support?

- Housing

- Health

- Education

- Support services

- Employment

- Income and asset building

- Civic engagement

COMMUNITY NEEDS ASSESSMENT REPORT OUTLINE

Once you have gathered all your information, it's time to tally, compile, and review. Look for common themes, request, and concerns. This report can give you a greater view into your community at a glance. Just like the questionnaire you develop, you want to make sure the report is reflective of the information you want to collect.

Assessment Report

Organization Name

_____

I. Overview of Needs Assessment and Key Players

Community

_____

Dates of Assessment

_____

Project Partners

_____

II. Methodology

The following methods of data collection were used:

☐ Surveys   ☐ Interviews

☐ Case Studies   ☐ Statistical Data and Reports

☐ Focus Groups

III. Participation

Respondent Demographics

_____

Survey Participants

_____

Focus Group Participants

_____

Case Study Participants

_____

IV. Assessment Strengths and Limitations

Strengths

Limitations

V. Key Findings

Data

Gaps in Service

Community Strengths

Community Challenges

VI. Recommendations

Recommendations

Next Steps

Program Proposals

Conclusion

FINDING A SAFE SPACE WITHIN PEOPLE

Safe spaces in your community must be ingrained as a part of the culture. And culture starts with people. People may often find themselves stuck in a hostile environment in which they feel unsafe. This can be because of hostile attitudes, stigmas attached to their identity, or just because of misunderstood interactions or cultural differences. In most cases, an uninformed, desensitized person or organization will create a lack of safety and acceptance.

It's vital to growth and safety that when you are navigating that space, you:

1. Begin to look for other LGBTQIA+ people who may occupy that space.
2. Seek out allies and create alliances with them by allowing them to know you.
3. Seek out your mentors for support and ask for coaching on next steps.

If you are fortunate enough to be able to identify other LGBTQIA+ people outside that space, it's important to develop that support system and keep them up to date. This will be harder in some places more than others.

I'll keep it real with you—if you work in an unsafe environment where most of your team or community partners don't appreciate you or may use your sexuality against you, you may need to evaluate if that is the culture in which you wish to invest your time, your effort, and your energy.

However, don't forget there is power in numbers. If you can find a few other LGBTQIA+ people or allies, and you're able to connect with them, develop a support system, and develop a great friendship or dialogue, you are creating safe spaces within the members of that group.

As a space safe coach, I was hired by a West Coast CEO to

come in and provided one-on-one leadership training and staff development training with a new director who was having trouble building trust with his new team of managers. The CEO was troubled that the skills that made his new director shine were not useful in managing his team. This was becoming increasingly evident by the incoming complaints to HR:

"He is a great guy, but he is power tripping."

"He doesn't know how to talk to people."

"He micromanages."

"He doesn't trust any of us."

These were just a few of the comments. Threats of resignation had been made by staff, and people complained they didn't feel a safe space to express their concern directly to this new director. I learned that the new director would have weekly meetings with all his managers and their staff to review every aspect of each team member's performance. Then there would be another meeting with managers the next day to discuss their programming. Meeting staff of his choosing one-on-one, without informing their superior, was common and often encouraged by the directors.

I came in to meet with each team member one-on-one and then the director to assess the discord. When questioned, the director believed it was helpful and necessary for him to direct his teams directly and daily. The staff believed he was micromanaging them, and the managers felt they were stripped of their authority by the way he talked to them in meetings, changed assignments, and gave them orders in front of their teams. However, the director believed he was being assertive and taking leadership.

I asked both the director and the staff if I could sit in on the next meeting, for note-taking purposes. Everyone agreed. As the meeting started, I observed and began recording without saying a word. It was about an hour and a half of the director speaking and the rest of the team simply reporting in. When the director had a question, he would often ask a manager. Then before the manager could finish, he would answer it himself before the manager was done speaking, and cut other people off mid-sentence. He often spoke of his years of experience as a social worker and made sure everyone else knew it.

What was most troubling was that this group was made up of Black and Brown LGBTQIA+ community organizers in their twenties, hired for their expertise in reaching out to their own community in the city they were actually living and working in. Telling this group of community members how to reach out to people in their community, and how to do their job better, was off-putting to most. The disconnect could not be more real and jarring.

After the meeting, I discussed these points one-on-one with the director. He pushed back, saying he was not pushy or bullying his staff, and that he provided everyone a fair chance to speak. I disagreed and asked if I could playback the audio so he could hear himself. He hastily agreed.

As his own voice played back, I watched his face contort. He would flinch when he got loud with his staff or cut someone off, and I could feel him getting uncomfortable at the sound of his voice. When I stopped it, he gave me a deer-in-the-headlights look.

"Yes, sir," I said. "This is you and this is what your team hears every day."

He'd had no clue. "Wow, I sound like a jerk," he admitted.

He had thought he was helping by taking the lead, figuring the team wanted it that way, without asking them what they wanted.

Then he asked why I had been counting out loud as the audio was playing. I explained that I was counting each time someone tried to speak up and he cut someone off—four times in ten minutes. I left the tape with him to play in private.

When I returned the next day, we played it from start to finish, and walked through what could have been done better. I coached the director in meeting with each staff member one-on-one. He shared his newfound discovery of himself and promised to do better by inviting them to provide feedback and providing a safe space to do so. We practiced positive self-talk, the power of sharing the mic, and leaving room on the agenda for others to speak. We came up with ingenious ways to assure there wasn't just one mic and one diva! It was simply making sure each staff member provided an item to the agenda that was important to them. Most importantly, however, I wanted to ensure that the team felt a safe space to share and express their concern. Unfortunately, after a six-month follow up with his team, it was reported he fell back to his old ways after just three weeks; micromanagement increased and HR reported about 70 percent of his team members quit.

Oftentimes, in dismantling misconceptions and stigmas alone, we discover that the person blocking our efforts simply has an ill-informed belief. We can change the misconceptions of others if we provide the opportunity to build a relationship, have a conversation, and have respectful interactions with one another, no matter how difficult it may be.

Here are a few tips you can follow in your journey to creating a safe space with your team or community members:

BE CLEAR WITH YOUR WORDS

When I'm working with someone in the LGBTQIA+ community, sometimes I may not know exactly how to address them. Whenever I'm unclear on how to address a transgender person or nonbinary person by their pronouns, all I do is simply ask. "Excuse me. I would like to address you properly and respectfully. What pronoun would you like me to use?" This is simple, easy, and has worked every time.

Your words can either interfere with or elevate your intentions. Your everyday language should reflect your feelings of acceptance and inclusivity in the spaces you occupy. Communication is key to building some of the most rewarding and deepest relationships. If you don't know, just ask.

SEPARATE YOUR FEELINGS FROM OTHERS' FEELINGS

It's important not to take everything personally. When working with the community or working in teams, you're going to be met with resistance, opposite opinions, and disagreements. Not everyone will agree or have the same definition of a space safe as you do. That's okay. These are perfect opportunities to create partnerships, coalitions, and learning opportunities. A great way to respect other people's feelings is to check in on your own and, most importantly, to be aware of what may trigger you.

CELEBRATE INDIVIDUALITY

I have a friend who has become quiet during our weekly dinners, and I've been wondering what is going on. I finally figured it out. Because our group is staunchly democratic, we are often so busy touting our political views that we don't bother to ask anyone else about theirs.

My friend has a few conservative political beliefs and has started to feel more and more isolated in our group. Individuality has strengths when it comes to collaborating, and we all know how integral collaboration is. If we had been more verbal about the positive aspects of political diversity, we would have never ostracized him to begin with.

We always are going to live in a world full of different opinions and viewpoints, but we need to make sure that we carve out spaces where people feel free to express their opposite views. In a safe space, there is an appropriate setting for debate and a place to exercise our beliefs, which can often lead to masterpieces of discussion and deep conversation.

Many times in debate and conflict, we have an opportunity to defend what we believe, but also to hear the reasoning of what other people believe. This dialogue is extremely valuable in building partnerships through difficult times. It also creates an opportunity to learn.

ESTABLISH A PERSONAL CONNECTION

Focus on being a leader who is accessible, receptive, and sensitive. It shows people that you care and that they are appreciated for what they bring to the table.

Here's a tip I got into when I first started speaking publicly in my career: meet people personally as they're coming on-site or into the establishment (pre-COVID, of course). Especially if you're going to be speaking at an event with many people, having a personal interaction—no matter how briefly—with people one-on-one allows you not only to build a personal connection but also to relax, speak more freely and comfortably, and exchange energy. I promise this tactic will leave you feeling like a star.

Never undervalue personal connections and relationships. When you need to have negotiations or discuss tough issues, a personal relationship with your audience will come in handy. On your journey, people will be as equally tied to your vision as they are tied to having a personal connection with you. Both relationships must be fostered properly. I can't tell you how many times I've gotten up to speak, fearful and trembling until I focused in on the smiles of people I had spoken to earlier.

When giving a talk, I make eye contact with the mothers whose sons visited a center I worked for, or who read an article I wrote. I can see the LGBTQIA+ manager who expressed to me, just minutes before I stepped on stage, how connected he felt to me regarding our experiences. I refocus on the outreach worker who anxiously but excitedly greeted me when I came on-site. I recall the person who helped me make my coffee by pointing to the sugar. Focus on personable experiences with your group as a way to talk to them directly.

START AT THE TOP

Be purposeful about taking inventory of your own attitudes and beliefs. Be introspective. Write them down. Then, let your day-to-day actions reflect those values.

Remember, you *are* a safe space. Therefore, there is an opportunity to create a safe space everywhere you look! Jump on the bandwagon with me and put the effort into making that a part of your social culture and lifestyle.

After I left the church as a kid, Christopher Street was my safe space. I could go there and be the insecure, naïve loner that I was at that point in my life. I was allowed to sit there by myself and soak up the atmosphere of inclusion and acceptance, watching the different groups of gay, lesbian, trans, and queer folks listening to music, dancing, and voguing up and down the street. Without fail, within a few minutes, someone would approach me and start talking. Before I knew it, I was instantly part of a chosen family who accepted me for exactly who I was in that moment. And that's the kind of inclusion I want for you, as well.

In creating safe spaces, incorporate other people's vision into your own and study how they may serve each other. It is integral to take the best pieces of each represented party and mend it into one cohesive vision. Yes, the goal is to create a safe space, but what are we coming together to accomplish within that space? This is where you start.

Once everyone is seated at the table and we begin to share our thoughts and ideas, it is essential to *use* the ideas that support the purpose and mission of the safe space. Should you have to say no to a particular idea, be sure to do it in a way that respects that person's voice and experience. They are still the experts here. Their ideas are still very valid, but just may not be the right ideas for your specific goal at the moment. The truth of the matter is, you will not always see eye-to-eye, but you have to find a way to do it tactfully.

Building safe spaces won't always be a nine-to-five job. Many times, community planning and organizing take place outside work hours. You must be personally invested, especially when working hand-in-hand with the community, translating their vision, and inspiring new community members and team members alike.

MAINTAINING YOUR MOTIVATION

Speaking of the endless hours involved in community leadership, I also want to address burnout with you.

Have you ever made big plans for your life, only to fail to act on them? Or maybe you started with a bang and kept your motivation for a few days, but suddenly lost interest? It's incredibly easy to lose motivation after the initial excitement wears off. But if you want to be successful, it's important to keep going. And not lose motivation.

Let's look at six ways you can lose your motivation and how to refocus your energy on getting it back!

1. THE PLANNING PHASE IS MORE FUN THAN THE EXECUTION PHASE

Sitting alone at night and making plans for the future can be an exciting time. I definitely remember being a kid with big dreams. Everything seems possible because you're only limited by your imagination at that point. However, when the sun comes up in the morning, it's time to get busy. It all seems a little more daunting and less enjoyable when it's time for the real work to start. So always remind yourself there needs to be a plan with achievable goals you're working toward, or it's just a dream.

2. YOU LOSE TRACK OF THE END RESULT

Remind yourself of the prize at the end of your journey. Visualize how it's all going to be when you've reached your goal. You should feel an immediate boost of motivation. In my case, if it's opening day for a new drop-in center or space, I visualize the community partners, the community members, the space, and most importantly the "we did it moment" and the lives we are going to change!

3. YOUR GOAL DOESN'T SUIT YOU

Many of us choose goals that are acceptable and praised by the world at large. It might be going to a certain school, getting a certain job, or buying a house or a fancy car. Sometimes these goals are tied to what we want to do in the community. Maybe your goal is totally mismatched to your real desires or temperament. It took three months at McDonald's for me to realize that it was not for me. The bottom line of making someone else rich wasn't always a big motivator for me to start with. Not working with the community seemed unfulfilling and dry day in and day out. Pick goals that match your interests and abilities, but most importantly, pick goals that excite you.

4. YOU FEEL UNCOMFORTABLE AND AREN'T DEALING WITH IT EFFECTIVELY

Of course, it's uncomfortable to do anything new. Whether it's creating a new income stream, creating a safe space with no money, or speaking truth to power, it's going to be uncomfortable. It's important to deal with this discomfort effectively. When I first began speaking, I would be so terrified that I would give speaking opportunities away. I would literally look for a reason why someone else was better to speak than me. Then they would speak and I would swear I could have done a better job, kicking myself all the way home. Expect to feel uncomfortable. Have a plan for working through it. If you're making changes in your community and progress in your life, discomfort is the norm. One of the greatest lessons I learned was to get comfortable with being uncomfortable. Earth shattering, right?

5. YOU HAVE TOO MANY NEGATIVE THOUGHTS

You're not ever going to finish that book, why bother? You're never going to publish. People are already doing it better than you. No one is interested in your queer Brown boy story. Negative thoughts are paralyzing. Negative thoughts will make you rationalize that you should quit and go home. Though it doesn't always feel like you have control over your thoughts, you do. You can choose what you want to think about. Take control of your thoughts. And catch your inner saboteur, as RuPaul would say. Catch negative thoughts and redirect your focus to something more positive. Even if it means telling your inner saboteur off, do it! And keep it moving. It takes time to develop this ability, but it will become second nature with practice. The key is to notice quickly that your thoughts are going off the rails and call your inner saboteur out.

6. YOU'RE STUCK IN YOUR OLD HABITS AND ROUTINES

Yup. I'm thirty-eight and I can attest that the older you are, the more challenging it can be to break out of your old patterns. We find comfort in our old routines, and our brains become hardwired to repeat them. In order to stay fresh, you'll need to create new habits and routines if you want to change your behavior and your results. When I feel stuck, I identify one habit that is getting in my way and one habit I need to create to help attain my goal. Put your time and energy into dealing with these two items. When you're successful, tackle two more.

*   *   *

Now that I've shared my six, which of these six reasons applies to you most often? Is there another reason you fail to sustain your motivation? Motivation and willpower are always shifting and changing.

Expect that your motivation will falter sometimes and be prepared to deal with it. Focus on creating habits that will take you to your goals; habits can reduce the need for consistent motivation as they become the norm.

ALLYSHIP AND SAFE SPACES

The importance of allies cannot be overstated. During the last few years, we have heard the term "ally" a lot. It's often used to describe a partnership between people who share a set of beliefs and who seek the same goals. Not long ago, the term "allies" was used more commonly to describe nations who supported and defended each other when the interests or well-being of either was threatened. Today, the term is often used to identify individuals "who position themselves as advocates working toward ending discriminatory action against marginalized groups."[11] Allies most times are *not* members of the marginalized groups.

As Dr. Waajida L. Small says, "More than ever, advocacy is more than just talking, and allyship is more than just speaking out against injustices."[12] It's about taking action in the moment to call out the wrong you witness in a space to prevent it from happening again.

Let's take a look at some effective ways to be an ally, and some actions that can help create an inclusive safe space for amazing community work to flourish.

11   Waajida L. Small, "Allyship at Work: How to Turn Intentions into Actions," *Idealist*, February 24, 2021, https://www.idealist.org/en/careers/allyship-at-work-actions.

12   Small, "Allyship at Work."

WHAT ALLYSHIP LOOKS LIKE

Allyship in the community is about recognizing the privilege that members of majority groups have in society—and using that privilege as a tool in the dismantling of systems and processes that prevent local community members from having equal opportunities. This will look different in different communities, but here is a set of three core behaviors[13] written by Dr. Waajida L. Small that make for good allies:[14]

1. **Knowledge and awareness:** No, it is not possible for you to understand the lived experiences of marginalized and minority groups. But it is possible—and necessary—for you to educate yourself on what these experiences may entail. As an ally, you should strive to deeply understand the mechanisms that cause discrimination as well as what "institutionalized racism" is. It is also your responsibility to be aware of the role the majority plays in perpetuating discrimination, as well as to have an awareness of your own privilege and how you can use it to be an ally.

2. **Communication and confrontation:** Knowledge is not enough. You should be able to share that knowledge by educating others. Go beyond simply being an informed bystander by opposing and exposing discriminatory actions.

3. **Action and advocacy:** Do what you can to support and promote marginalized groups. Actively participate in activities geared toward dismantling institutionalized oppression. Do so publicly and engage in and with people and platforms working toward these same goals.

13 Nicholas P. Salter and Leslie Migliaccio, "Allyship as a Diversity and Inclusion Tool in the Workplace," in *Diversity within Diversity Management Vol. 22*, ed. Andri Georgiadou, Maria Alejandra Gonzalez-Perez, and Miguel R. Olivas-Luján (Bingley, UK: Emerald Publishing Limited, 2019), 131–152, https://doi.org/10.1108/S1877-636120190000022008.

14 Small, "Allyship at Work."

Allyship is more than just wearing certain colors, posting online, joining a protest, or telling your Black, LGBTQIA+, or female friends about the latest rally you attended. It's about taking action when people make racist, sexist, homophobic, or transphobic comments. It means creating space for people of color, the LGBTQIA+ community, and women in senior leadership roles to grow. It means requiring transparency—and if you learn of bigotry, unfairness, or sabotage, have the empathy to feel a duty to speak up.

Real allyship is centered on what you do. You can create a space that has zero room for discrimination by filling your environment with values of acceptance and fairness and openly rejecting any behavior that contradicts those values, even when it means acknowledging the role you play.

AVOID PERFORMATIVE ALLYSHIP

People won't always be watching, and you won't always have a big audience, but that doesn't mean the work is not happening or being effective. Founder and former President of International Justice Missions, Gary Haugen, states the need to stay focused beautifully: "The victims of oppression and injustice don't need our spasms of passion, but our long obedience in the same direction."

A lot of the real work goes on behind the scenes, takes time, and many times goes publicly unrecognized. To be 100 percent real, that is how it should be. If you are invested for the long haul and want to be a part of the real long-lasting change, don't always expect a pat on the back. If you're only looking for recognition, then your allyship is only performative—and therefore not welcome.

WHAT PROMOTING LGBTQIA+ EQUALITY AND INCLUSIVITY REALLY REQUIRES

Securing LGBTQIA+ equality and inclusivity is about ensuring justice, fairness, accessibility, and a sense of belonging. Here are some great actionable steps that you can take to bring about lasting change in your space, from a recent *Ladders* article by Elaine Lipworth:[15]

- **Shift your mindsets.** Change will not happen overnight. Understand you are in it for the long haul and commit to it.

- **Commit to learning.** Learning about the past is incredibly important. Understanding the history of oppression will inform you of why things are the way they are today, and how you can work to prevent oppression from being repeated in the future.

- **Think about what it means to be a true friend.** Stand up for marginalized groups the way you stand up for your friends. When you see people being mistreated, speak up. In the workplace, make sure there is appropriate representation and diversity in the room when decisions are being made and promotion policies are formed to ensure equitableness.

- **Create a sense of belonging.** Dominant voices dominate the conversation. Be intentional about inviting other voices into the conversation, especially when decisions are being made.

---

15 Elaine Lipworth, "Allyship in the Workplace: What Promoting Racial Equality and Inclusivity Really Requires," *Ladders*, June 18, 2020, https://www.theladders.com/career-advice/allyship-in-the-workplace-what-promoting-ra-cial-equality-and-inclusivity-really-requires?utm_medium=referral&utm_source=idealist.

- **Advocate for the hiring and promotion of more Black people and other people of color.** Your leadership and workforce should be reflective of the communities you serve.

- **Channel hope for a better future.** Have the moral conviction and intolerance for racist and oppressive behaviors and instill it in others.

As you can see, LGBTQIA+ allyship is about carving out safe spaces that promote equality, which increases the chances of success for any person regardless of their sexual orientation or gender identity.[16] Many times, allies go through a learning curve as they evolve into better allies. Take a look at the stages below so that can you understand the allies in your life.

THE FOUR STAGES OF ALLYSHIP

Author and advocate Lily Zheng and clinical psychologist Inge Hansen share the different stages of allyship in their book, *The Ethical Sellout: Maintaining Your Integrity in the Age of Compromise.* These stages are incredibly valuable to learn while you're creating teams with allies, ensuring the right people are on board and at the level of allyship you genuinely need.

Each stage takes time to grow into and out of. The point is to value the journey from each stage and strive to go further. As you review the four stages Lily Zheng and Inge Hansen have identified, which best describes you and your allies? [17]

16   Nisha Kumar Kulkarni, "How to Be a Better Ally at Work," *Idealist*, July 6, 2020, https://www.idealist.org/en/careers/allyship-at-work

17   Lily Zheng and Inge Hansen, *The Ethical Sellout: Maintaining Your Integrity in the Age of Compromise* (Oakland, CA: Berrett-Koehler Publishers, 2019).

Stage 1 of Allyship: What Do I Do, Again?

You stay quiet and listen to what other people are talking about. You're new to this space and starting to learn about #Diversity, #Equity, and #Inclusion. You want to do the right thing, but aren't sure what that means or looks like yet.

Stage 2 of Allyship: I Don't Get It, But I'll Do It

You follow the direction of other people. They say show up at an event, you show up. They say speak up when you see something wrong, and you do. You can't articulate *why* you do what you do, but you hope you're helping.

Stage 3 of Allyship: I Get It. I'll Do It

You're a reliable figure at this point in meetings and events. You've built a reputation as someone that consistently rises to the occasion when asked. You can confidently explain the *why* behind what you do.

Stage 4 of Allyship: I Know Where I'm Most Needed. I'll Do It

You've built an understanding of power, access, and privilege into the way you work. You're not just doing as you're told, but also determining opportunities where you can make a unique impact and prioritizing them. You leverage your power within an organization to subvert inequity inside and outside it.

COMMUNITY RESOURCES

You really can't talk about allyship without the topic of community resources in the mix. It's important when making an ask to clearly state your needs—this especially includes when working with or recruiting volunteers. You can always try your luck at reaching out to other LGBTQIA+ communities, community-based organizations, local LGBTQIA+ college groups, LGBTQIA+ clubs or promoters, or other community centers that may not focus solely on the LGBTQIA+ community but offer LGBTQIA+ discussions or activities.

Another great resource in our community are aging LGBTQIA+ voices that are available for conversations or mentorship. Because of their time and experience, they have great lessons and connections they are often willing to share that can help steer you in the right direction. Value these highly important members of the community. They preserve and often pass on valuable historical memories to the rest of our community.

We need to be conscious of those who came before us and make every effort to be sure that our senior community members are equally represented at the table and across the community. So, when looking for community resources, be creative. They are out there, and they are waiting for a vision and a hope like yours. You just need to do the due diligence of finding, engaging, and listening to them.

I know I have said it repeatedly in these pages. Fair representation at these decision-making and community planning tables are a must. Growing up, I merely sat at the table many times and never spoke. Learn from my mistake and avoid the regret. Take your seat at each one of these tables, learn who is in the room and what the subject matter is, and resist every temptation to sit back and be silent. This doesn't mean you should come in ready to take over like that one director did; it means you should show up ready to share and give.

Speak with passion about what you truly believe and allow your values to radiate your worth. Do your best to be clear and to the point.

CHAPTER 6

Becoming the Best Leader You Can Be

"As my mom always said growing up, 'When you do something, do it con ganas.' To her, that phrase extended to the way in which my siblings and I not only pursued our careers, but to how neatly we swept the floor. So, whether you're early in your career and have to side hustle as a barista, or have finally made your way to the corner office—do it all con ganas [with desire]."

—ANALISA CANTU, CONTENT PRODUCTION ASSOCIATE AT JOPWELL

Since the world—and the community—is ever changing and fluid, the way we organize or manage teams or community members should reflect those changes in the community: being flexible, passionate, and inspirational, having unwavering intention, and always staying community-focused.

My goal here is to share, using the current practical tasks at hand to pass on time-tested organizing skills and life lessons.

BECOME A BETTER LEADER: FOUR STEPS TO BOOST YOUR EQ (EMOTIONAL INTELLIGENCE)

Most of us think of a leader as someone with a great deal of education and experience in a certain area. While knowledge and experience are important qualities, one's ability to communicate and work well with others is just as important to being an effective leader.

Fighting in the trenches as I rose through the ranks of the organizations to which I devoted my passion, skill, and expertise proved to be invaluable. To this day, even though I often find myself in leadership positions and in boardrooms, my heart is in those trenches with my community and community team members. Alongside my "boardroom" work, I also conduct street outreach to LGBTQIA+ sex workers, organize community events, coordinate HIV/STD testing, exchange dirty needles for clean ones, help to look for missing trans women, and provide company for young people losing their fight with AIDS or drug use. It can often be tough and heartbreaking, but by doing all of this work, on all levels, we fight *together* for the liberties of LGBTQIA+ people in our community and across the globe.

Leaders never leave their teams behind to sit somewhere else more comfortably. We must strive to be leaders who elevate others and inspire confidence in them so that they believe they can succeed and make a difference the way our ancestors, LGBTQIA+ pioneers, and community legends have. Like Bayard Rustin, who led a life of activism. Or Essex Hemphill, who performed an incredible act of bravery during his short life with his raw and brave writing. Our prime example of a trans leader and activist is Sylvia Rivera, who was a community rights leader, a transgender woman, and a veteran of the 1969 Stonewall uprising.

Being a Latinx LGBTQIA+ person who just shows up is not enough anymore. Being connected to the community and only taking from it is not enough. We need effective leaders to set the vision, inspire us to get moving, and guide us in carrying out the mission, providing tools, resources, and connections along the way.

As such, having a high degree of emotional intelligence (EQ) allows you to be able to inspire others to cooperate with you to accomplish a shared objective and vision. There are several ways that you can strengthen your interpersonal skills. Try these methods to dramatically raise your EQ and accomplish more together:

1. INCREASE YOUR SELF-AWARENESS

Self-development is the foundation of excellence. Before you can lead and inspire others, you must first understand your own motivations and behavior.

- Develop your vision by learning to listen to your inner voice, values, and dreams. Trust yourself. Try not to compromise your values to achieve a goal or for other temporary gain.

- Embrace passion by learning to be motivated by your internal compass rather than external forces and situations.

- Keep your energy fully charged so you can give your best effort. You can stay energized by taking the time to learn what activities re-energize you and which ones drain your energy.

- Respect yourself. Know the limitations of your body, mind, and spirit and strive for balance between your responsibilities in all areas of your life. It's okay to say, "No!" And respecting your own boundaries is okay. Just like my experiences with Timothy when I ignored this golden rule, not speaking up and not setting boundaries can put you in harm's way.

- Become aware of your flaws and limitations. Seek ways to improve yourself and be open to change. For example, one flaw of mine for a long time was feeling like I needed to do everything and be everywhere to represent the organizations or community I worked with. And I did it all—until I realized I could be so tired that I wasn't really present at all. When I was burned out, it limited how I used the talents and experiences of my team members. I had neglected my self-care by overextending myself in the name of my community. Don't do this.

2. TAKE RESPONSIBILITY FOR YOUR ACTIONS AND LEARN TO SELF-MANAGE

Owning your behavior, attitudes, and actions can raise your performance level as well as help you to build trust and authority with others.

- Seek the input of others. Ask how you can help them, or what you need to do differently to communicate more effectively and manage them better.

- Constantly check your actions against your values to make sure they're in alignment.

- Don't be afraid to delegate responsibilities and tasks. Be confident enough in yourself to surround yourself with talented, qualified people.

3. DEVELOP YOUR SOCIAL AWARENESS

Be aware of your own attitudes and the power you have to motivate others.

- Show genuine concern for others and learn how to actively listen. For instance, in my work with

LGBTQIA+ youth sex workers, my primary way of building trust was by showing up when I said I would with the care packages and packed dinners I said I would bring. I would talk about and listen to whatever they wanted to talk about that night. Consistency will create lasting bonds and foster a strong community bond that will work with you rather than against you.

- Give others a reason to support you and your vision. One way to do this is to let others know when they have done a good job and look for ways to openly recognize and reward them. This can be anything from acknowledgment of an idea to taking someone's ideas, working with them, and then giving them credit for the success. When I was growing up, knowing that I was being seen by people I admired furthered my desire to support them. And when I saw them succeed, I was so happy for them because it felt like we were invested in one another.

- Help others to buy into your vision by making them stakeholders in the attainment of your goals. Seek their advice when setting goals and making plans on how you'll achieve them.

- Help others to increase their abilities and fully utilize their talents by providing opportunities for training, mentoring, and self-development.

4. EMPHASIZE GREATER RELATIONSHIP MANAGEMENT

Learn how to bring out the best in yourself and others. Utilize everyone's best qualities and minimize their limitations with effective assignment of tasks and delegation of responsibilities.

* * *

Regardless of your education or experience, you can achieve greater success by learning how to use your people skills to fully harness the talents and energy of others. These strategies will allow you to increase your EQ and inspire others to fully enlist in your cause of their own free will.

As I have said many times, you are not born with leadership skills, but you can absolutely learn how to become a phenomenal leader. It is a lifestyle that you practice, one that becomes authentic over time as you learn, experience, and allow yourself to be mentored and supported by a guide who gives honest and timely feedback. You must yearn to be a leader.

I guarantee you *will* get better with time. Leaders are better equipped to make sound, quick decisions in high-pressure situations because of their experiences in many different circumstances during their lifetime. Good leaders eventually become immune to, or comfortable with, the pressure that decision-making brings, and intuitively make gut decisions on the fly every day. It eventually becomes instinctual.

THE POWER OF MENTORS

I was blessed enough to meet men like Alex Williams, Amistad Aromand, Thishin Jackson, and Shelton Jackson, who saw the drive in me that I didn't yet know existed when I showed up to that initial LGBTQIA+ community focus group.

These young men had experienced the effects of HIV, either directly or indirectly. They had all sorts of ideas on how they saw themselves helping the community and what they believed was the most effective way of doing it. When they met me, I was a shy kid with no sense of direction or any idea that I would one day immerse myself in a lifelong LGBTQIA+ safe space journey. This group of confident Black gay men formed a tight circle of brothers, and they took me under their wing and fostered my passions.

Some of the most valuable insight and lessons they helped me learn was to teach me what it means to be an advocate for the LGBTQIA+ community, along with the value of my voice and my lived experiences. They taught me that my experiences and my voice could never be taken away from me unless I allowed them to be taken away. To this day, I firmly believe your lived experiences are the foundations upon which your influence and stories rest.

When I first started coming out to people I knew, I attached my sexuality to an act. I thought, *I'm gay because I like to be with men instead of women.* I didn't understand that being gay embodies *way more* than your sexual partners. It also includes the social responsibility to your community and to anyone else who is different or "othered" by mainstream society.

My mentors encouraged me to widen my perspective and to live in my truth. They talk to me nonstop about self-worth and what it really meant to have confidence in myself. They taught me that self-esteem was not tied to how I dressed, what I looked like, what I could do for others, or even what others could do for me. It was about me understanding that I was valuable in the world and that my story mattered as much as the next person's. It was more about developing the confidence in myself to be able to mirror my personal pride every single day to all of the people who sought help from me. I learned that to model how others should advocate for themselves, I had to demonstrate that advocacy and self-worth in myself to the people I came in contact with every day. To find that self-confidence, I had to first look introspectively at who I was, and then tie who I was into who I wanted to become and what I wanted to achieve.

In *your* vision, ask: who is your ideal self? Once you have a vision of who you want to be, and who you are striving to be every single day, lean on that vision. Lean on the values of that *ideal* self. Isolate these values, choose to become concisely aware of them, and practice them.

Remember, it's important that you make a distinction between what is *your* mission and *your* purpose in *your* personal life, and those of your community.

Not every day will be a good day. Some days, one vision is going to look bright, and another day, not so much. On the great days, both of those visions—for you and your community—will be in alignment, working for you amazingly. The point is, you're not always going to be able to control all the elements that you want to control when it comes to bringing your creations to life. But make sure that you're investing your time into both your personal vision and your community vision, in that order.

EMBRACING YOUR UNIQUE SKILLS AND LEADERSHIP QUALITIES

I love talking about leadership because I have been practicing and honing those skills since I was a young boy. Growing up, I was always placed into a leadership role voluntarily and involuntarily, whether that meant cooking Thanksgiving dinner because my mom was working or keeping an eye on my rambunctious twin brother every night when she went to work. Leadership was instilled into me as a survival skill.

What I love about leadership is the ability to create other leaders. That sounds atypical in this day and time, but that desire to give back and mentor others truly drives me. I also strive to develop other leaders in a different manner, with even more intention, than the one through which I developed.

Of course, I was pretty fortunate in my experiences. Bill Orr, my first professional mentor at the HIV/AIDS community-based organization I worked for, gave me, a sixteen-year-old teenage boy with zero experience, an opportunity to become a part of his organization and his vision. He allowed room for me to make mistakes and stumble, but he also allowed me to make up for it and explain where it could have gone wrong and what may have been done better. He was always able to communicate his vision in a way that inspired me to want to do better. His ability to communicate his vision clearly and build partnerships allowed me to see allies in the most unlikely places.

I also wanted to be just like Amistad Aromand, the second manager for the project at the LGBTQIA+ center I started in. He was the epitome of a leader.

Amistad instilled truth and accountability in me every day. "You are a leader, Julio. You are the only Puerto Rican kid at this table. You need to show up. You need to educate yourself on the issues. You need to speak up. You need to represent," he reminded me very often. He gave me the tools and books, sent me to the trainings, had the hard conversations, and was empathetic with me. I admired him so much and always said to myself, *If I ever become a leader like him, I will have made it.* This is how my mentors fostered my personal and professional growth.

THE POWER IN TRANSPARENCY

Amistad, as I would come to learn, is an advocate who fears nothing in expressing what he believes. He is loud when he needs to be, always providing honest, in-your-face, and thoughtful truth that always makes you think more broadly about issues. He's also a kind person in how he manages his teams and people around him. He became the first person to unveil the power of transparency to me.

When he first started as a manager, I was a little hesitant. I didn't know who he was and was still heartbroken my first manager had to leave for personal reasons. I'm sure he sensed this. He invited me to conduct a safe space focus group with him to a group of fifty men recently released from prison. He disclosed, through vivid storytelling of his own life, how he, a young Haitian gay man, become HIV positive through a loving relationship with his partner. The room fell silent; eyes widened and mouths open. He gave freely of himself that day, fearlessly embracing every question thrown at him with beautiful honesty, in order to tell a personal truth of who and what he had experienced.

His honesty, trustworthiness, and bravery during this event made me even more loyal to him. He showed me that vulnerability can be strength, and that pain gives us an opportunity for the greatest of possibilities and connections to occur with other human beings. He also taught me that the man I am today is not the man I'll be tomorrow. In no uncertain terms, he reminded me that I had a voice, and I had a responsibility to use it. He held me accountable when I needed it most and reminded me that I could forgive myself. I admired his leadership so much I wanted to emulate him exactly.

Over the years, I have found it is vital to keep changing up your leadership style until you find something that works for you, your community, and your organization. The goal here is to not stop until you find that style that works for you and adapt your leadership skills as needed.

When I look at all of my mentors, I can see each part I took from each one and how I practice them in my own style. I believe what is different about my style than other mentors' styles is that I'm using my unique lens of experience and know-how as a queer Brown man to guide and inform my decision-making. I finally discovered that while I can admire great leadership, there was no need to completely imitate someone else. The knowledge I had and my drive to help others was more than enough. Guidance is always key.

I simply had to learn how to be comfortable in my own skin, and hope that I could inspire others with respect and my authenticity.

My story is unique to me, just like your story is yours alone. When you find yourself in charge of a team, allow your people to be the leaders of their own expertise and guide them to write their own scripts. Done right, this will increase morale, create magic, and stoke ire.

EIGHT WAYS TO INSPIRE YOURSELF AND OTHERS

Inspiration is a person or thing that moves or motivates you to action. I often call it the seed you plant to ignite passion. It's hard to get anyone to care about something that does not move them emotionally or morally. In order for them to care about an issue or cause they may have never heard of, it's up to you to inspire them to care.

Inspiration is everywhere. Although it's not always as easy to spot during challenging times, it is always present. It's important to remember that inspiration means different things to different people.

WHAT TO LOOK FOR WHEN INSPIRING OTHERS

Since you may not always know what others like, it can sometimes be difficult to get through to others and inspire them. Rather than showing others what inspires you, strive to teach them how to look for the spark they seek. When they know what to look for, they'll be able to see inspiration every place they look for it. Consider:

1. Breaking down a larger object into fine detail and studying that detail carefully.

2. Analyzing a conversation for subtle nuances that might give you ideas to work with.

3. Looking more closely at something you generally only see from a far-away distance.

4. Using a writing or drawing prompt to get your creative thoughts flowing more easily.

5. Thinking, looking, or listening outside of the box to see new ideas and opinions.

6. Asking others about what inspires them and looking for the hidden beauty in those things.

7. Taking a class in something you've never done before or a language you want to learn.

8. Traveling to a place you've never been to see the culture and beauty there.

OPEN YOUR EYES TO INSPIRATION

When you teach someone how to locate sparks of inspiration or interest on their own, they'll possess that skill for the rest of their life. Then they can find their own excitement wherever they are: at work, at home, or on the go. It's a simple strategy that's great for the creative type, or for anyone who feels stuck in a rut.

Finding that creative spark is within your reach, if only you make the conscious decision to leave your comfort zone in favor of new experiences. Be willing to make mistakes and look silly by trying new things and living life to the fullest. Creative inspiration is as close as your next decision to try something new.

When you step out of your comfort zone, you'll be different from the crowd, but you'll live a life filled with colors, textures, and a richness that so many fail to experience. Decide today to try something out of the ordinary or find a hobby that allows you to decompress, and see what creativity flows from you and to you when you do.

You deserve all that life has to offer. Why not make a new choice?

LEARNING HOW TO LEAD AND HANDLE CONFLICTS AND SELF-DOUBT IN A NEW ROLE

Successful leaders lead. They take what is given to them and enhance, grow, or create more from it. They nurture and grow it, taking it to a place it has never been. The most simplistic definition of leadership to me would be taking what you are given, no matter how limited that may be, no matter how small the resources, and moving forward, improving upon it. In other words, leave a situation better than how you found it.

If I were to take away the often rewarding aspects of leadership, like respect, influence, access, working with amazing change makers, and being able to create, you would essentially be a problem solver of all sorts of conflict. Learning how to resolve conflict with a cool head is essential to your suitability to lead.

When I became a manager for the first time, it took me some time to really be assured of myself and my new role. Mentally, I had to make the switch from staff member to the leader of the team. Now, I was responsible for supervision, the development of each team member, and the quality of each program. This meant that all my old friends whom I started with as my coworkers were now reporting to me. At the start, it was all fine. I tried to stay the same cool, chill team player who just went with the flow, but soon there were conflicts. Conflicts that arose because boundaries began to be pushed and I now needed to hold the same team members accountable.

To recreate working relationships, I began to have one-on-one meetings once a week with each team member to build something new, starting with expectations. We discussed their goals, programming, and what support they need. Through action and follow through, I wanted to represent a safe space and a resource. Three months into these one-on-one meeting, there was a shift in great energy that you could feel, and the one-on-one meetings became requested instead of required. Because I knew the team as a peer, I was also able to have real conversations regarding my negotiable versus nonnegotiable needs.

Every level of success or leadership comes with its own level of conflict that you are now responsible for as a leader. When I first started speaking and presenting on community organizing or advocacy, I found many of my mentees who were new to leadership often experienced new challenges in their new roles, as it related to their teams and community members.

I learned through my own trial and error that you always have to deal with conflict if you want to advance in life, both in community organizing and professionally. And here's the kicker: at the next level of leadership, there will be a whole new body of challenges and conflicts for you to solve.

In creating LGBTQIA+ safe spaces, we must be fluid but also have the ability to be a stabilizing force and steadfast in our principles. That meant I could not get frazzled, even when I felt that I failed, or the work wouldn't move forward.

When I think of failure today in regard to community planning, I would define it as failing to create a safe space for the community to be their authentic selves at the table. Failure would be creating a plan and goals without ever including or consulting community members. I will admit that I have come up short and missed the mark more than enough times, but I learned from the experience every time. And I know that putting in the effort to examine mistakes both small and great would only strengthen resolve and decisions in my next endeavor.

Use the setbacks and failures of the people who came before you as a roadmap to achieving your future goals and not wasting time duplicating mistakes. The only way that you could *totally* fail is to fail to learn from your own lived experiences and fail to learn from your ancestors' experiences—good, bad, and indifferent—that you were blessed to encounter. When you do fail, figure out what didn't work, what did work, and what could have been done better.

A lot of times, we are not consistently or consciously aware of the inner saboteur who talks to us. This inner critic becomes a beast who thrives on negative beliefs when we feed it regularly with our doubts and fears. This is where positive self-talk comes in: "I am not a failure. I am not a loser just because this piece of the puzzle did not fit." "I am deserving." "This is not the end of the world. Just readjust and keep moving." Then I modify next steps based on the lesson learned and move on to the next goal, mission, or activity.

THE BEST LEADERS ARE SMART THINKERS BUT NOT KNOW-IT-ALLS

If you are in a leadership position over a group, congratulations! You have been handed an awesome responsibility. Again, it's vital in your role to assess your people's capabilities, trust their ability, and allow their voices to be heard in the room, regardless of whether you know the answer or *believe* you know the answer.

As the good and fair leaders we believe ourselves to be, we must consistently be aware of when we need to step back and when we need to step forward. Everyone, if provided the space, wants to step up. In my experience, I've sat in countless conference rooms, HR offices, or exit interviews with excellent workers and talented people who were afraid to speak up or say one word just because the highest-titled person in the room couldn't seem to understand that it was not about them for the moment. If you are unable to create or unwilling to share the space for others to flourish and grow, this will be off-putting and morale-busting to the most passionate people on your team.

Along with direction and space, the best support you can give your team is encouragement, clear direction, and acknowledgment for their efforts and ideas. Don't be afraid to say, "Great job!" or "Please let me know how I can support you," or "Please keep me updated on the amazing work." For your own self-care, and to keep morale up, resist the temptation to be the end-all-be-all.

Encouraging others to speak can also improve your accountability and that of others, especially when you invite pushback and discussion. When we have an impact on other people's lives, we need to foster a sense of responsibility. As LGBTQIA+ leaders, we need to be able to check those we mentor and also be open to being checked by our own peers. This includes members with more experience, whether that's an older individual or an accountability partner. They will be able to help us see the bigger picture and move us out of harm's way when we think we know it all! They're great ego-checkers, too.

Maybe you've heard the expression that "you don't know what you don't know." When I am in the middle of a project with my team and a conflict arises, a tool I use is called "retrospective listening." With this method, each member can communicate their concern while the other member listens and determines what their thoughts and actions would be if they were in the speaker's shoes. "Would my actions and choices remain the same?" the listener thinks. "Perhaps I'd feel the same way." This allows for more compassion and understanding so the team can work together toward a resolution. At the very least, it allows for a new level of understanding.

When you allow people, especially the quieter ones, to speak, you can almost see their confidence increase with time. "Oh, my gosh, how *would* I deal with that, if I was him?" It presents a level of understanding that each person hadn't thought of prior. You don't know what you don't know, right? But now you *do* know how it feels to be in the other person's shoes.

Let's face it. On top of your leadership role, you're going to have a lot of other responsibilities. So, again, take the time to develop your passionate mentees, community members, and allies so when they get in a room with other people who challenge them, they can stand their ground.

SIX WAYS TO BE AN APPROACHABLE LEADER

Leaders are sometimes seen as intimidating or powerful, but a good leader has the ability to make everyone in the room feel as if they are of equal value, with the right to be seen and heard. They make other people feel comfortable speaking their opinions by creating a safe space for them to do so, and giving them confidence in their own voice.

In other words, leaders are *approachable*.

So how do you become more approachable as a leader, and in your everyday relationships?

1. MAKE THE FIRST MOVE

Avoid standing on the sideline. It's always important to make sure that you are initiating the first contact and the first conversations with people you want to get to know or partner with.

2. LISTEN CAREFULLY

Not only is it important to know your community's stance on the issues at hand, but it also shows them that you pay attention. They will see you as being a lot more approachable in the future. You want them to feel safe and comfortable to come talk to you about things that are important to them, with the understanding that you should be able to give them valid, valuable feedback.

3. SHARE

When you are willing to give something of value, your team is more likely to give you something back. Don't be afraid to share lessons. Don't be afraid to share experiences, both good and bad. And don't be afraid to share your expertise around knowledge that may help them perform better, and that can also be applied to other areas of their lives.

4. CONNECT ON A HUMAN LEVEL

There's the potential to make connections everywhere in the community and on your team, so try to find personal connections and activities that you can foster, like hobbies or other activities where you can connect with people in your community on a human level.

5. ALWAYS THINK ABOUT YOUR NONVERBAL CUES

While it's important to be aware of how you look and portray yourself out in the world, always be conscious of what nonverbals you're giving out to those you lead and the community. People look to you during a time of stress or crisis, so keep your cool. We should *always* remind ourselves that we are stabilizing forces in a world that is always changing.

6. ASK GOOD LEADING QUESTIONS

Always have a list of questions in your mind about topics that you can ask team members, community members, allies, and partners in the community. Be prepared to engage, and always remember that open-ended questions are better for allowing people to engage and to keep conversations flowing. In this way, you can learn and gain valuable information from your community.

TO SUM IT UP

Ultimately, I have found that I can get through anything negative at work if I don't tie my self-worth to my projects. I understand that any project can fail, but I can't personally fail unless I quit. Newsflash: I am *not* a quitter, and neither are you. This outlook has grown on me throughout the years. I have had to change that negative self-talk to gain the confidence it takes to succeed. Sometimes it is as simple as silently telling myself that my opinion matters as much as anyone else's in the room, and that I bring as much value to the world as anyone else, regardless of where I am at right now.

I believe that God has a plan for me—and that the God of your understanding has a plan for you—that is outside the realm of what anyone can control, including ourselves. Growing up in church instilled in me that I was one of God's children, and that meant that I could rely on God's promises instead of my own imperfect abilities or the abilities of others. It gave me the foundation to accomplish the dreams and plans that God has for my life.

Keep your head up and take the next step into your purpose boldly and fiercely.

I hope that by sharing myself with you, you are inspired to take some of my life lessons and apply them at will. That's why in the next part of this book, I'm sharing eleven leadership lessons I wish I had the opportunity to learn much sooner than I did. Over time, these have guided me to success—some were passed down, others learned by experience, and some are still developing. Like life, take what applies to you and recreate it to serve your purpose and who you are as an individual. Allow your experiences—the good, bad, and indifferent, your trauma, your joy, the experience of love and empathy—to guide you and lead you. Allow the lessons of life you have experienced to serve as a defining and inspiring light in the world.

Repeat after me: "I'm here and I'm worthy because I have a mission to achieve. I have something amazing to do on this earth!"

Of course, the best way to discover your purpose is by throwing yourself into new experiences. However, learning key leadership lessons for an empowered mind, body, and soul and a connected, thriving community will give you a competitive edge. I hope you will benefit from them now.

Newark (2019)

Queer Black Lives Matter march in West Orange, NJ (2019)

PRIDE City Hall Celebration in East Orange, NJ (2020)

National Trans Visibility March in Washington, DC
(International Transgender Day of Visibility, 2018)

AIDS United—AIDSWatch in Capitol Hill, Washington, DC (2017)

Puerto Rican Day Parade celebration at Newark City Hall (2020)

LGBTQ+ Commission swearing-in ceremony at Newark City Hall (2020)

Puerto Rican Day Parade in Newark (2021)

Mom and me on LGBTQIA+ Anti-Bully Awareness Day in Jersey City, NJ (2015)

Part II

Eleven Leadership Lessons for an Empowered Mind, Body, and Soul and a Connected, Thriving Community

"People will never fight for your freedom if you have not given evidence that you are prepared to fight for it yourself."

—BAYARD RUSTIN

CHAPTER 7

Lesson #1: Set a Clear Vision for Yourself

"Remember, goals are stars to steer by, not sticks
with which to beat ourselves."

—BARBARA SMITH

You will learn early on that vision is shareable, but a vision for you must start with you first. Before you can support a bigger community's vision, you need to understand what part of your vision will play a role in the community. And that means *you want to have a clear vision for yourself and your ideal future*, along with how much of yourself you are willing to give. You need clear boundaries so you are not always conforming to everyone else's visions for *who they think you should be, what they think you should be doing,* and *what the world should look like through you.*

As an LGBTQIA+ leader, it's important to define the role we want to play in our own lives, our communities, and on the world's stage. We need to do this for burnout's sake, for capacity's sake, and simply for the overall fairness of who we are and what our reputation represents to ourselves and our community.

When you're presented with a new opportunity, take a moment to ask yourself: *How is my personal vision going to play a part in the overall vision I've been asked to assist with?* In assessing your community, organizing your community, and working directly with the people in the community, everyone has their own unique vision. Some may know it and be aware, but others may not be so aware but still have a vision worth sharing when prompted. And, trust me, they are all going to give you their vision and opinion, whether you ask or not.

Although it is important for the overarching vision of the community to align with your vision, the details, timelines, and circumstances can change along the way, and that is okay. That's life. Whether everything goes according to plan, or something unexpected happens, what role you play in that change is ultimately yours.

WHAT'S THE DIFFERENCE BETWEEN MISSION AND VISION?[18]

We've heard these three words—mission, vision, and values—so often in business meetings and presentations that our eyes gloss over and we forget that each word represents a separate and distinct concept for creating safe spaces.

The difference between a vision and a mission is that a vision focuses on the *future*: on what we hope to achieve as the ultimate end goal. The mission focuses on *today* and what an organization or group does or needs to do to maintain alignment with these written ideals as they move closer to achieving that ultimate vision or mission. For instance, you and the community may have a long-term vision of creating a safe space and opening an LGBTQIA+ center. The end goal is opening the doors to a new safe space. The missions involved in getting that done may look like this:

18   Adapted from Brit Skrabanek, "Difference Between Vision and Mission Statements: 25 Examples," *ClearVoice,* February 14, 2020, https://www.clearvoice.com/blog/difference-between-mission-vision-statement-examples/.

- **Mission 1:** Identify a free community space that's LGBTQIA+ friendly.

- **Mission 2:** Recruit and put a call out for volunteers.

- **Mission 3:** Create a core group of people who express a special interest in being involved in the planning process.

- **Mission 4:** Identify the community gatekeepers for a meeting.

- **Mission 5:** Identify allies who can help supply the center or space with resources.

Knowing the difference between a vision and a mission and communicating your ideas and intent clearly are vital in leading people and creating safe spaces with a sense of purpose.

As content strategist Brit Skrabanek shares, "The lines especially get blurred with vision and mission. But when it comes to the drive and direction of your group today and tomorrow, you don't want to have trouble seeing when you're behind the wheel."[19] This means that you should know which immediate tasks need to be completed in order to get you one step closer to where you need to go. For people to have a sense of direction when following you, they must know what comes next. You must be clear when talking about your goals.

While many groups commonly use mission and vision statements interchangeably, it's important to have both. One doesn't work without the other, because having purpose and meaning are critical for any group or safe space. Let's figure out how to establish each of them.

---

19 Skrabanek, "Difference Between Vision and Mission."

ESTABLISHING A MISSION STATEMENT[20]

Your mission statement drives the purpose of your safe space and provides the reason why it should exist on a day-to-day basis. It is what you do, the core of the work, and from it comes the objectives and what it will take to reach those objectives. It also shapes your safe space's culture.

Mission statement questions will often look like this:

- What do we wish to achieve as a group or organization?

- Which populations do we serve?

- How do we serve these populations?

You can quickly see how a clear mission statement can motivate a team to take action toward a common goal because they all started at the same place and they are now working together to reach the same identified end-goal.

But if you have a weak mission statement, or none, that can have the opposite effect. You won't be going anywhere if your team doesn't have both a map and the motivation to move.

This is the exact opposite of what you want and need in creating safe spaces, so make sure you have a solid mission.

WHAT IS A VISION STATEMENT?[21]

A good vision statement inspires growth, both internally and externally, provides direction as well as personal growth for those who are a part of your team. As Brit Skrabanek writes, "A strong vision helps teams focus on what matters the most for their community. It also invites innovation. A purpose-driven team

20 Skrabanek, "Difference Between Vision and Mission."

21 Skrabanek, "Difference Between Vision and Mission."

envisions success as a whole, because they know what success means"[22] for their safe space.

A lack of vision, much like the lack of a mission, will create a disconnect and stop any forward movement. Remember, the vision is the ultimate end goal.

Imagine your safe space or LGBTQIA+ center years down the line. Now imagine what you wish to achieve, your dream for the future, your success as a community—all of these should be captured in the vision statement. Keep in mind that the statement should only include the vision, not an actual step-by-step plan for implementing solutions. And stick to the specifics!

Some of these questions can help you clarify your vision:

- Where do we want the organization to go?

- What can we realistically achieve?

- What problem does the organization intend to solve?

- What are the changes we believe the organization can make for individuals? And for the community?

- How will things be different if the vision is achieved?

- What phrases or keywords describe the type of organization and outcome we want?

IDEALISTIC AND REALISTIC GOALS AND VISIONS

I have an idealistic vision of what I would want if the world was perfect. This vision includes no hate crimes, equality everywhere, fair access to housing and clean water, fixing global warming, and ending teen suicide. However, to be a true visionary, I have to work

22 Skrabanek, "Difference Between Vision and Mission."

with the reality of what's in front of me at that moment. This is important to remember: sometimes, you have to downsize your missions or break them into more achievable phases. You have to develop that sixth sense, extra-sensory perception of knowing how to adapt your goals and handle your resources in the wake of the ever-changing variables in the world.

Your mission is the path you are going to take and the strategy you are implementing that will carry out the vision.

Truthfully, you have to keep both vision and mission in sight at all times during your journey. Theodore Roosevelt said, "Keep your eyes on the stars, and your feet on the ground." In essence, your vision should be far-reaching and big, while your mission should be manageable and achievable.

It is easy to get so consumed with the beauty of the end goal that you fail to concentrate enough on the not-so-beautiful tasks of executing the plan. It is also true that the exact opposite can happen. When we only see the details and urgency of the day-to-day tasks, we risk losing our overall vision for the future and its beauty. It really is a delicate balance and a dance that can be mastered with time, trial and error, and patience.

Mentorship is key to learning how to maintain that balance. It's crucial that you have a mentor or someone from whom you can seek advice, guidance, and counsel. All great leaders or role models need to be able to have honest, heavy, and real conversations with someone that they can trust as a confidante. We all need someone who can be true and giving, brutally honest, and who doesn't fear our title. Someone who can be real with you and doesn't sugarcoat their responses. They're the ones who will tell you the truth when you need to hear it the most. They're the people who can help you, as my grandmama would say, "Be put back in the correct place."

WHAT'S YOUR ROLE AND LEADERSHIP STYLE?

There are many leadership roles that you will have the opportunity to play, and all of them are necessary. Often, you will have to play more than one role at any given time. The most important thing is to consciously decide what kind of participatory role it will take to get your team across that finish line, what you will spend time on, and what you will not.

The pastor from my first church is a perfect example of someone who was able to juggle lots of moving parts. He was the founder and president of a theologian seminary and his own ministry, as well as a businessman, counselor, and leadership coach to other church leaders. He taught a weekly class in his seminary, wrote countless books, and traveled to preach the gospel. And on Sunday, he attended all three services.

He was the shepherd who had a vision, who knew each member's name, and knew where the church was going. He developed many to lead with him. And despite his use of the word "sissy" that one day at the pulpit, he consistently preached that we are all leaders ordained by God as part of a royal priesthood created for a special purpose. His commitment was to make sure no one was ever left behind. He served from the place of a shepherd by using this method, developing leaders to lead because this worked for him. And he created countless church and community leaders and supported many social movements with leaders who went on to continue to affect change to this day.

The reality is that the whole team must be balanced and paid attention to. Neglecting your people and mainly focusing on processes alone demotivates your best team members and sows seeds of doubt, both in the leader and in the team being led. Take the time to engage your people first. Seek their input, use it, and then move forward with them as partners.

Management encompasses many things. As the example of my pastor demonstrates, it may require you to play every role, or play several at once. What I learned as a manager is that since you're inevitably going to be required to play every single role at some point, it's important that you don't allow the idea of titles or positions or rank to ever get in the way of how effective you can really be. Use the opportunities to be seen as a role model and to create teachable moments.

I also think of my very first manager and now brother, Amistad, who, for me, was a passionate leader who led by example. He showed us what he wanted from his team and staff by doing it first and making sure he modeled it for us. He took responsibility for his team in every scenario, especially in failure. This allowed the team to take chances and be creative without fear of messing up and getting blasted for it. Amistad has a by-any-means-necessary type of leadership style, which is the opposite of my pastor, who would turn the other cheek and pray about it. Both were equally effective, and both are equally needed.

When you are approaching leadership and working with teams or the community, you have to decide what type of leader you are going to be in each possible setting. Are you that radical leader who grabs a mic and jumps on stage and represents from the front, proclaiming the call to action? Or are you the leader that is about mentoring other potential leaders and supporting the structure and movement from the middle or the back?

It's vital to ask yourself, "How am I leading? How am I using my voice? My resources? My connections? My network? My expertise? My experience? My energy? My access? And how am I using and displaying empathy, compassion, decisiveness, and love?" No matter what leadership style we choose to use, if it does not allow us to grow and push us to be uncomfortable as a result of that growth, we must find another style. Life is about learning, creating, and remolding ourselves. Growing never stops and learning never stops. Not for effective leaders.

A lot of this, of course, is contextually dependent. Learn how to utilize your skills and understand that sometimes, you may need to be a little of everything. We may not need to take the mic all the time, but there will be moments when we all need to get up and say something. You may not be a servant-type leader at heart, but there will be times when you will need to move to the back to make room for others to move to the front and develop their own leadership skills and voice.

Not only should you recognize which type of leader you are, but you should also be able to recognize the same traits in the people you lead. It is a beautiful sight when those you mentored can speak the very words that you yourself were prepared to utter. There is a power and a synergy in being of one accord when delivering a message, and this is the benefit of effective team building and leadership development.

CHAPTER 8

Lesson #2: Stay in Your Lane and Protect Your Peace

"The richness, beauty, and depths of love can only be fully experienced in a climate of complete openness, honesty, and vulnerability."

—ANTHONY VENN BROWN

Staying in your lane means understanding and appreciating the qualities each team member brings to the table and making space for those qualities to surface. One of the big lessons I have learned when assembling a team for creating a safe space is understanding that I am not the expert on everything. Some of the biggest challenges I've faced in my career have been moments when the leadership above me or executives I worked with were left unchecked and took over the whole process to serve their own goals or ego.

Sometimes I still must remind organizational leaders of this truth: "Yeah, you've been doing this work for two decades, but you need to create room for others in the room to speak. And not only speak but support what it takes to make it actionable. Even though your experiences may have served you then and you may have accomplished great things, what's taking place today will need fresh eyes, fresh ideas, and fresh input from the community."

Not staying in your lane or respecting other people's roles communicates a lack of confidence in your team or community members. You inadvertently build resentment among your most faithful and send the message that seeking guidance is a weakness and speaking up is a waste of time. That's a slippery slope to losing momentum and having your best advocates check out and walk away.

So how do you keep yourself in check as a leader and stay in your lane?

Stay aware of how often you interject, when you interject, and whom you tend to interject the most around. Are they Black? Are they women? Or are you an equal opportunity interjector?

Before you speak, ask yourself, "Am I the only expert in the room?" Chances are, you are not. Many times, we do this out of habit, or because we want to move the meeting along, but other times, we do it because of internal biases that make us believe this is okay and acceptable. Other times, we're deluded into thinking that we know the right answers to every question and every situation, when that's simply impossible. Stay in your lane by trusting your team and the experts you have access to.

As LGBTQIA+ people, community means a lot. We value the connectedness of having a family. We value the connectedness of celebration. We value the cohesiveness of experiencing and overcoming trauma, and being able to gather in places where we feel safe and where people look like us. But we also value individuality, and we embrace the fact that each and every one of us is unique. We value that each and every one of us is here to serve a unique purpose, and that our traumas and celebrations provide an unbreakable connection to one another.

As leaders, we must absolutely respect the value that each of us bring to the table or conversation, but also be able to take a seat to allow others to be experts, as well.

PICKING YOUR PARTNERS AND PROTECTING YOUR PEACE

I have a duty in writing this book to provide fair warning when it comes to protecting your peace and advocacy goals from ill-intended energies or simply saying yes too often to things you don't want to (or don't really *need* to) participate in, or events that will overlap with your personal calendar and rest time.

If you are a passionate community leader, advocate, or community gatekeeper, your reputation will grow as you provide a voice and support to those who follow you. With this growth will come invitations and requests to partner with all sorts of organizations and groups. Many times, these organizations or groups are seeking you out because of your influence, great skill set, followers, or connections to the community. My advice when it comes to protecting your peace is to take extreme care and be selective when it comes to who you work and align yourself with.

An effective way of doing this is by asking around and talking to current and former staff members or volunteers about their own experiences with these organizations. Ask what they found to be most rewarding and most challenging about the culture and leadership. Also always ask if they have any advice they would like to give you—and listen carefully. Even going online and googling the group or organization's name can turn up some information or reviews. The goal is to get honest and real feedback so that you are fully informed about where you are investing your time and energy. There are many great organizations, businesses, and groups out there, but please beware that for every great organization, business, or group, there is a terrible one—so be careful.

The call to action that the Black Lives Matter and Me Too movements presented forced the true colors of inept and privileged leaders to be seen. Far too many organizational leaders, companies, and businesses who serve and profit from communities of color fell silent during the call for solidarity. And trust me, that lack of action was heard loudly in Black and Brown communities. Leaders were conflicted in stating the obvious, that they were choosing inaction over action in order to prevent public backlash and—drumroll, please—a loss in sales and overall profit. These organizations failed to aid the Black community and the women working for them, groups that are directly affected by these two movements. In the end, when leadership chooses to politicize and ignore human rights issues, it highlights a privileged perception, which creates a lack of empathy to truly understand the movements at hand and issues to be addressed.

The unwillingness to talk about inequality for Black and Brown people in this country and in our workplaces, or diverting attention or conversations to something more *comfortable*, is a tactic that further feeds racism. It destroys the historical lenses of trauma experienced by communities of color, making peace of mind impossible. How do you sit in peace if you do not feel understood, seen, or heard?

Here are some common questions to ask and some red flags you should be on the lookout for before joining up with any group.

- Does the organization or group have a history of **boldly** standing with the communities they serve? If so, then how, when, and where?

  Red flag: If they are always "staying neutral" and following what everyone else is doing.

- Does the organization's leadership and board look like the community members it serves?

  Red flag: If the organization's workforce is 99 percent Black and Brown, serving a community made up of 100 percent people of color, yet there is little to no people of color in leadership roles and board members.

- Does the organizational leader hire their family or friends for key roles?

  Red flag: If family is working directly for other family members in high roles, often violating their own family/friend company policy, many times with the blessing of the board. (This should raise eyebrows around accountability. Nepotism is real and is often created to secure power. This setup is normally used by leaders who don't necessarily represent the community they work in or their workforce. These family members tend to be placed in power centers like operational and financial roles. Nothing creates an us-versus-them culture quicker than this. If you see this, it should ring alarms.)

These are just some questions you should always ask. Do your homework, and if you have other questions, be sure to ask before you commit. Be good to yourself in choosing who mentors you and influences your development.

CHAPTER 9

Lesson #3: The Power of Peer-Led and Peer-Driven

Cultivate a Deep Sense of Trust Among the Team and Community through a Universal Lens

"Optimism is a muscle—it gets stronger with use."
—ROBIN ROBERTS

A safe space, purpose, or mission created *by* the community and *for* the community ensures greater success than one created through the leader's ideas alone. This is because buy-in and ownership lets the whole group emotionally invest from the start of planning and discussion. These talented and amazing community members are already believers of their own vision and their own ideals. You are simply providing a platform for the voices of their experiences to be heard and valued by putting them into action.

Once you listen to their ideas and beliefs, you can immediately start using them as a driving force for the overall goal and as motivation. As one of the leaders, it allows you to play the supporting role in enhancing your safe space.

If a safe space is peer-led and peer-driven, it is specifically representative of the community it will be serving. Even the language that the community uses is going to be used in the safe spaces planning.

PEER-LED AND PEER-DRIVEN

The peer-led, peer-driven model is about empowering your community to take charge. It's about giving the people responsibility for the safe space that they want to be a part of by amplifying their voices and giving them a platform to drive. It's about providing LGBTQIA+ people a voice at the table, creating a space in which they can find support, and ensuring they are part of a collective identity to create change and safe spaces.

Creating a structure for your safe space is just one way you can use the peer-led, peer-driven model of engagement. This model empowers community members to lead and drive the organizing efforts for creating a safe and welcoming space. The key to having the right community members at the table is to create an advisory core group of volunteers and community members who have expressed interest in helping you build a safe space and who agree to meet regularly.

Prior to coming up with all sorts of ideas, rules, hours of operations, and activities, set up a meeting with core members and bring their voices to the table to inform these decisions. This is how you start to meet the community where they are.

An example of making a peer-led, peer-driven event come to life is an annual LGBTQIA+ Hallows Eve party our team organizes in New Jersey. The core group members choose and lead: theme of the party, flyer designs, venue location, and the DJ. They do Facebook promotions, sell tickets, pick the food, pick the host, pick the entertainment, pick the ballroom categories, and pick the prizes. They even decorate the space and clean up. It's all about meeting the LGBTQIA+ community where they are by providing support the whole time and creating together.

Whenever I'm called in to work with an organization to create a safe space, my primary objective is to assure that the community voices are at the table. This is done by ensuring that a peer-led, peer-driven model is at the center of my thinking.

This is the best information that you will be able to get or pull from the community experts in your field. This also creates an early buy-in. Studies have shown that groups or people who are invested in the startup of a safe space are more likely to be invested in the success of that space.

So, when creating your own unique peer-led, peer-driven missions, it is important that you keep your feelings and your emotions in check. Vision, ideas, and dreams are extremely sensitive topics for everyone involved. Sometimes, we begin this process envisioning our own ideas until we invite new voices to the table. This can create a challenge, but do not forget challenges also create opportunities for dialogue, discussion, and idea-sharing.

CHAPTER 10

Lesson #4: The Importance of Utilizing the Community's Experience and Gatekeepers through Partnership and Coalition-Building

"We need, in every community, a group of angelic troublemakers."

—BAYARD RUSTIN

It's critical to utilize LGBTQIA+ gatekeepers and partnerships in every aspect of community or organizational planning. By incorporating the community's past experiences, including their successes and failures, you'll be better able to plan for the future. Gatekeepers are community members who are seen as leaders in the community, and they hold the keys to public opinion. They are often the ballroom house parent, DJs, promoters, influencers, and entertainers. They're also bankers, retailers, and teachers. Gatekeepers come in all gender shapes, sizes, and professions.

Community gatekeepers are popular opinion leaders, members of the community who have influence over a greater part of the population, simply based on their social status or forward-thinking ideas in the community. They have a following who respects their values and input, and they are highly celebrated community members. Try having any substantial community event or local initiative without their input or involvement, and you will absolutely limit the effects or reach of your effort. They can also serve as great ambassadors, messengers, and bridgebuilders, making them the ideal advocate.

A gatekeeper can help you a great deal. As an example, here's a conversation I had with a powerful gatekeeper, Legendary Mother Tyra, about a local kiki scene:

Legendary Mother Tyra: Chileee, they said you're going to make it mandatory now to attend your group to go to the kiki function or ball practice.

Me: Yup. I want to keep the kiki scene going, especially on Boot Camp Wednesday. But as you already know, in order to do that, I need to make sure that we are testing our girls and getting more of our kids on PrEP. Since they either don't want to, or we are not offering it effectively, we need to try something new. I refuse to see thirty-five people walk in on Wednesday just for boot camp, stroll past our group, and not one gets tested. Or better yet, only five visit the LGBTQIA+ center. So, I'm thinking about a few options. Ohhh! And I got read! One of the kids cussed me out because I told him he had to attend group.

Legendary Mother Tyra: What? Who read you?

Me: Who else? Sabrina and Michael, the ones who are never here.

Legendary Mother Tyra: I'll talk to them. I get what you're saying, Julio, but these kids haven't known anything but this kiki spot for a few years now. If you cancel it or make it immediately required, many won't come back. It's going to be like a few years ago when the other center shut their doors suddenly and we had nowhere to go. They gonna read the fuck out of us in person and online, and remember, some work before this kiki practice and others are coming from school. So, I'm just saying, let's relook at this.

Me: True. I think we need to reprioritize our priorities honestly. It's like kiki practice has taken center stage, and that can't happen all the time. And for people who work and go to school, I get it. But it seems like we have to talk to our community again and look at reprogramming so it works. You're Legendary Mother Tyra. What do you think?

Legendary Mother Tyra: Listen, you know I know the girls. Give me a few weeks, maybe three or four, to get people used to this new rule. I'll come up with some ideas with some of the house members for you. I'll also talk to them about making sure all the girls are tested in each house.

Me: I can do four weeks, love. I know you know the community and they trust you. Work your magic. Also, please let our members know we don't want to disrupt this safe space time. But we need to balance why we are here and how we can continue to keep this space open. Let's promote our vision and make sure we are on the mission of reducing HIV in our community.

Legendary Mother Tyra: I think we should offer services on the mic before, after, and during the kiki practice, and require everybody new coming to talk to a PrEP counselor before they can hit the floor. In a fun and super dope way.

Let me handle it from the mic. I think we have to include the messaging in the kiki music, and we may need to look at our hours too. If the girls are running late, why not just push an hour back? At the end of the day, Boot Camp Wednesday is the only safe space a lot of them know. By doing this, Julio, we can avoid the issues that will arise if they feel their space is going to be taken from them. You can trust that.

As you can see, Legendary Mother Tyra is a highly respected and involved gatekeeper who knows the needs of her community and is not afraid to speak up and challenge ideas. A lot of what we do in the LGBTQIA+ community cannot happen unless we have partnerships as allies in the community. While it is important to work with folks individually to amplify their voices, partnering with people who have a proven track record of showing up and bringing about change is the key to gaining credibility in the community. Let's please read that last line again. You get that through your gatekeepers.

I can't talk enough about the importance of being able to recruit and utilize gatekeepers as your ambassadors. They already have a rapport with the community through their own rights and presence they've spent a lifetime establishing. The best thing about gatekeepers is they also have an inside connection to other LGBTQIA+ social networks that may be too difficult to engage yourself.

Instead of only asking the gatekeepers to help you, or only celebrating them during certain times of the year, take great care not to overuse or abuse your access to gatekeepers or popular opinion leaders. Their responsibilities in the community are great and tiring. Make sure you care for them. Check in with them periodically and make sure they are okay, asking if there's anything they need from you.

BRIDGING THE INTERGENERATIONAL GAP IN THE LGBTQIA+ COMMUNITY

When we talk about community gatekeepers, it's important to bring up the intergenerational gap that we see within the LGBTQIA+ population. This can be a whole book in itself, so I won't attempt to dive into the subject as an expert, but I do want to make a note of it here.

Now, what is the intergenerational gap? I'll define it here as the gap in the sharing of history and cultures that exists between younger LGBTQIA+ people and older LGBTQIA+ people.

As a society, and I believe even more so with gay men, there is a perception that you lose value as you age, almost as if the older and more mature you are, the more you become invisible. The problem with making people invisible is that we risk missing their contribution, what they can bring to the table in terms of experience. We lose institutional memory and become more prone to misplace historical facts on a community level, since our LGBTQIA+ local histories are often not well documented or stored in one central location.

An organization that I admire for preserving Newark LGBTQIA+ history is The Queer Newark Oral History Project. A community-based and community-directed initiative supported by Rutgers University-Newark, QNOHP is dedicated to preserving the history of LGBTQIA+ people and communities. They work tirelessly to tell and record the community's stories in the words of its trailblazers and legends by collecting audio-recorded oral history interviews. Their website features countless interviews documenting the lives and recording the history of Newark LGBTQIA+ leaders, advocates, and community members.

When we lack this curiosity, we begin to lose our grasp on our history, our traditions, and experiences that have welded this community together. When we don't ask questions or seek knowledge of our past, we further widen the intergenerational gap between our shared history.

UTILIZE YOUR PARTNERS AND KEEP BUILDING RELATIONSHIPS

The saying "never go in alone" is true in many areas of life but is never truer than when creating a safe space.

It's vital to utilize what partners and coalition building efforts you already have in place so that you are not depleting all your own resources or struggling to make things happen on your own. Partners can be your favorite local printer, local organizations, other advocates, a local official, LGBTQIA+ school alliances, DJs, your local LGBTQIA+ commission, the PRIDE Parade association, and basically anyone who wishes to work with you. Also, anyone you take donations or money from is a partner.

Be strategic in how you utilize your resources in the community and with whom you partner, and make a concrete effort to reach out to your partners regularly, developing sound relationships through updates, checking in, and one-on-one meetings. Remember: everyone loves a free lunch and good company!

As LGBTQIA+ leaders and advocates, it's imperative to reach out and offer assistance and support to others without waiting for an invitation to do so. This does wonders for relationship building and creating great synergy through collaboration. We must continue to do the sometimes tiresome but rewarding job of reaching out ourselves to create those partnerships and coalitions. In the future, I believe this piece of the puzzle is going to become a more solidified and prolific part of movements in general.

CHAPTER 11

Lesson #5: Invest in Your Team's Development by Identifying and Providing for Their Needs

"Like racism and all forms of prejudice, bigotry against transgender people is a deadly carcinogen. We are pitted against each other in order to keep us from seeing each other as allies. Genuine bonds of solidarity can be forged between people who respect each other's differences and are willing to fight their enemy together. We are the class that does the work of the world, and can revolutionize it. We can win true liberation."

—LESLIE FEINBERG, AUTHOR AND TRANSGENDER ACTIVIST

Where am I sleeping tonight?

How do I ask for help?

How do I tell my boss I'm homeless?

In 2001, these questions had already awoken me for the day. They started off as a small whisper in my mind that only got louder as the day turned into night. I knew what needed to happen.

I slowly trekked into the drop-in center, partly from the lack of sleep that haunted the soles of my feet, and partly from the dread of having the people I admire learn that I was homeless.

I felt like I had failed somewhere and perhaps I wasn't the role model everyone believed I was.

I wanted to ask for help but had no clue how to bring the subject up. I didn't want my manager or my team to look at me as a client, even though I had all the same needs as a client at that moment. I needed a support system; I needed guidance and most importantly shelter. And yet, here I was, an "advocate" who helped other people ask for help, struggling and unable to ask for help myself.

Luckily for me, my manager scheduled weekly one-on-ones with me to discuss everything from work goals, professional goals, and life goals. He was always asking, "How is Julio doing?" "How are you feeling?" "How are you?" And the most important question: "Is there anything I can help with or that you're concerned about that I am unaware of?" By asking these questions and following up with me, he created a safe space for me to speak and share with him what could be barriers to me being safe. I finally told him the truth about my current situation, and it felt like a ton of bricks lifted. I suddenly didn't feel alone anymore. This gave me added fuel to believe that I was just going through a phase of difficulty and that I was still a role model and worthy to serve my community.

It is important for leaders to get to know each of your team members, understanding what their weakness are, assessing their maturity level and what motivates them, and even their future hopes and dreams. One way to create trust and build a team bond is to create time to get to know who the person actually is. The only way you can do that is to understand each member's perspective, goal, and what inspires them.

Many teams that I need to organize are made up from the community themselves, and all have unique needs that fall outside of the spectrum of their role. But if those needs aren't addressed or even acknowledged, their work could very well be affected.

UNDERSTANDING THE DYNAMICS WITHIN THE COMMUNITY

It makes sense that a leader should be informed of the challenges their team might be experiencing on any given day, when they are asking things from their team members. But how, as a leader, can you help meet some of those physical and material needs?

There have been times when I referred team members to places that help out with rent. I have referred team members to a mental health counselor or substance-use detox programs. I've worked with a new mom who also worked for me because she needed to go to WIC (Special Supplemental Nutrition Program for Women, Infants, and Children), but she didn't have any time off. Her bank account was in the negative, and she was afraid to ask for it because of how her boss in her last job reacted to her request with her child. I only learned any of this by asking how she was and if there was anything I could help with as she nervously walked into my office.

Get to know your team on that level. Being a leader isn't only making sure things work, or only about the mission and vision. Many times, being a team leader requires that you take the time and intention to build a house—your organization and community—where your team feels at home, like they belong.

Yes, this takes work. No, it is not easy. But is all worth it at the end.

CHAPTER 12

Lesson #6: Don't Miss Happy Hour

The Importance of Decompressing

"If I wait for someone else to validate my existence,
it will mean that I'm shortchanging myself."

—ZANELE MUHOLI, SOUTH AFRICAN ACTIVIST AND ARTIST

For as far back as I can remember, my mom has always been such a hard worker. Between all the jobs she would do during the day and the bartending at night, I can't think of another woman who has worked as hard as she has. I am sure many of us feel this way about our moms.

One of the most treasured memories for me growing up was waking up on Saturday mornings, getting dressed, and going to the Doobie shop with her and my brother. The day just seemed brighter for some reason. I can still smell the strong Bustelo coffee wafting through the air, watching my mom and other countless women getting their hair done in the tightest Doobie wrap by these beautiful, and I mean *beautiful*, Dominican women on Broad and Market. My twin brother and I sat at the front and watched all the women coming in and out, and I would steal glances to watch all the flamboyant male hairstylists in the salon. They were funny, loud, and fit right in.

After the salon, my mom would take us to get our hair cut and then onto the NJ Transit to Kmart or an afternoon movie. If we caught a movie before four in the afternoon, tickets were $3.50 each. After four, they were $10.50. Needless to say, we were always on time, our pockets packed with our favorite candy, of course. Before we headed home, we'd go by Burger King or get a McDonald's Happy Meal. Those days were the best, just the three of us enjoying each other's company until it was time to head home. When it was not a pay week and money was tight, my mom took us to the Newark Library, Newark Museum, or my grandma's house, always creative in her endeavors to take us out. These were also her only ways to get us out of the projects for a while.

To this day, I value and still remember those moments. Even after a hard two weeks of work and stress, my mom made sure we had the opportunity to decompress, relax, and have fun with her. Going to the matinees and getting haircuts was such a treat because it allowed us to leave our normal surroundings and have our mom to ourselves for a whole day.

I cannot stress the importance of decompressing, relaxing, and taking time for yourself and your family. Take the time to create memories and moments that allow you to heal and restore.

As an advocate and as a leader or role model within your community, you must look after yourself, your well-being, your mental health, your physical being, and your emotional health. Please be aware of how you are channeling, resting, and recuperating. Be aware of how you are feeding your soul and your spirit. Be aware of how you are gaining knowledge.

The most effective advocates are advocates who first advocate for themselves so that they have the ability to advocate for others.

CREATE YOUR OWN RITUAL

One of the things that I do to decompress and relax from the pressures of the world is practice unplugged weekends where I cut myself off from all social media. That means putting your phone down and not making yourself accessible by phone or email. It is a little radical in this day and age, but I learned that unplugging at least once a month really allows me to be alone with my thoughts. If you have a partner, this is especially important.

What your decompression ritual looks like will be highly specific to you. Personally, I'm a big fan of how-to books, so decompressing for me means reading a really good book on a Saturday or Sunday night, and curling up on the couch with a snack and some wine. I also like to check in with my mentors and confidantes. I'm able to talk to them about what's going on in my life, vent about my frustrations, and seek guidance or just a few laughs.

My favorite way to reconnect with close friends is planning small gatherings at home. I love to plan dinner nights, movie nights, wine nights, card nights—anything that doesn't take too much work, but that will also allow me to stay within my own comfortable environment, looking the way I want while being connected with friends or family to chill.

It is important to decompress and practice self-care to revitalize your mission and your vision. It increases your ability to engage and be creative. And finally, it allows you to pour energy into what matters most to you. A great deal of passion is needed when you're attempting to inspire folks to connect with you, grow with you, and build with you on an idea, cause, or issue. In order to ignite the spark to fully express your fire, you must make sure you have the energy needed, and that means being aware of your self-care practices.

PASSION BECOMES DISASTER WITHOUT ENOUGH ENERGY

Passion for your goals alone isn't always going to energize you and carry you through to the finish line. Of course, passion is essential to have in community advocacy, or in anything you do, because the work itself can be exhausting no matter how much you love it. At the beginning of a new initiative or idea, take extra care in knowing and being aware that you will wake up some days with a vision that has not been fully realized yet and, in many cases, not even started. Use this as a motivator, knowing it's always like that at the start for you and everyone else.

However, your passion will de-energize you at times. Passion requires an enormous amount of energy that must be channeled and cared for properly. Because you believe in your cause, that cause requires fuel to grow. So plan for some downtime so you can re-energize.

The truth is, we only have twenty-four hours in a day to pack in everything we want to accomplish, and that includes sleep. Life's pace seems to be increasing all the time, but the reality is there is only so much time to fit in all the things we are passionate about. It is a constant balancing act between work, fitness, family, friendships, and domestic life, just to name a few.

EIGHT WAYS TO RECHARGE AND LEAVE WORK AT WORK

Now more than ever with COVID life, I find it easier to physically leave work than leave work behind. With Zoom and access to digital work at home, it is way too easy to go home after work and still ruminate on the day's events, replaying frustrations and feeling heavy with everything that seems to weigh on your shoulders. You must manually make time to decompress, however that means for you.

I'm going to share what I have found that works for me. It was a matter of going online and researching great options and ideas. Take a look at what I have and see if something speaks to you directly. If not, perhaps my list will spark some ideas within you for your own search. Also, FitDay, a healthy lifestyle website, has a great list of ten easy ways to decompress:[23]

1. **End your day with a glass of good wine.** Red wine has many antioxidants and is actually pretty good for your health. Don't overdo it on the alcohol, though, and make sure to drink water before and afterward. If you are not twenty-one yet, skip the wine and think about another treat you find indulgent. Is it a piece of dark chocolate? Is it a hot cup of Starbucks? For me, it's red wine, Franks pizza, and yes, some reality TV. *The Real Housewives of Atlanta* and *Potomac*, please.

2. **Take a kickboxing class.** What better way to decompress than kicking a punching bag or another (padded and willing) class member? Local gyms tend to have discounts for new members, and Groupon is always a great place for discounts, too! I'm personally blessed to have connected with my local kickboxing gym, whose owner is a fit expert and an LGBTQIA+ member who agreed to provide self-defense classes for our transgender population and fundraisers. If you don't want to leave the house, you can also purchase your own at-home kickboxing bag and sign up for an online virtual class. YouTube is great here if you don't want to pay!

3. **Meditate in your bedroom and light some candles for ambiance.** My favorite music for meditation is the yoga station on Pandora, but YouTube works great. You might be surprised at how many soothing recordings are out there, from classical music to binaural beats. Turn on

23   Nicole Kennedy, "Take a Break! 10 Ways to Decompress for a Better You," *FitDay*, https://www.fitday.com/fitness-articles/fitness/the-health-benefits-of-music.html.

your relaxing music, take a deep breath, and try to relax for at least five minutes. Slowly build up in five-minute increments until you can meditate for thirty minutes. If meditating is not for you just yet, start off with your favorite slow jam. Nothing is more soothing to me than a vinyl of Sade.

4. **Put on your favorite movie (or trashy reality TV show), make some popcorn, or grab the ice cream.** My partner hates when I turn on trashy reality shows (because he gets sucked in), so it's become my guilty pleasure when he's not around. Some of us also have that favorite old movie that takes us back to a safe place or a happy childhood moment. For me, it's *Home Alone* during Christmas or *The Goonies* during Halloween. Whatever it is for you, find it and enjoy it!

5. **Make a new iTunes playlist.** I like checking out playlists on various music and lifestyle blogs to find new bands and local talent. The website 8tracks.com is perfect for this. New music and oldies are great for long drives and home workouts, as well. I live with my AirPods in, so it's important to me to have music that can help me channel how I'm feeling at any moment. It's a way for me to step away for a moment mentally, when I'm working out, strolling through the streets, or if I simply want to feel at peace.

6. **Create a vision board for your goals.** This is powerful! Instead of using Pinterest, do it the old-fashioned way. Get your scissors and clip some images and words from magazines. Tape these to a poster board or pin them to cardboard and place it in a special environment for extra motivation for your goals. I keep mine right on my bookshelf next to my desk at home. I have no

choice but to see it every single day to remind me of the amazingness I'm striving for. Do not overlook the power of a vision board and the energy it creates when you need to be inspired or reminded of the greatness you're meant for.

7. **Give yourself a facial with at-home products.** My favorite products are those that I can make using ingredients in my kitchen. Coffee grounds are a great natural exfoliant, and milk is great for balancing skin tone. You can also go to the pharmacy with a set budget and pick up a few skincare items. Do this only if you don't feel like creating a science experiment in your kitchen. My weekly favorite is The Cocoa Dream Hydration Mask. It's a quarter of an avocado, one tablespoon of cocoa powder, and one tablespoon of honey. Mash away and apply for thirty minutes before washing it off. The glow is official.

8. **Get to bed an hour earlier than normal.** Sleep is important for a healthy lifestyle, a regulated immune system, and a happy mood. Try turning off your tech devices an hour earlier than usual and climb into bed. Turn off your TV and just relax for a few minutes before shutting your eyes. Bonus points if you keep your phone in another room at night and move the TV out of your bedroom. There is something magical about not allowing the outside world to interrupt the peace you find in your bedroom.

By following some of these suggestions and coming up with a few of your own, you'll soon create a healthy weekly routine of self-care and lower your stress levels, both at home and at work. Remember, start small and stay consistent! You deserve it!

CHAPTER 13

Lesson #7: Stop Trippin'

Leading with Empathy, Boundaries, and by Example

"Openness may not completely disarm prejudice,
but it's a good place to start."

—JASON COLLINS

It can be emotionally and mentally exhausting to over-empathize with everyone you meet in the community. As you hear the stories, you sometimes feel as though you're literally reliving those experiences. Especially if you have experienced trauma similar to theirs, it's common for this to happen. This is why boundaries are so important to you and the community.

The word "boundary" can be a bit misleading. It conveys the idea of keeping yourself separate. But boundaries are connecting points and limits that provide healthy rules for navigating relationships, intimate or professional.

As a newbie in homeless work, I worked my butt off and I wanted to be the best case manager I could be. I wanted to show the most compassion to each newly homeless person or family I helped with intake and found sheltered for. Maybe because I knew the feeling of being homeless and homeless with my family. I compromised my better judgment and broke rules—like letting people in after-hours into their beds, allowing them to shower with no supervision because we were understaffed, or providing mail after mail hours because they worked, etc. Of course, this got me called to the boss's office where, without breaking his stare from his desktop, he explained: "Don't ever over-empathize with the clients."

I took it as, "Don't place yourself in their shoes or care too much." When I asked for clarity, he said, "Have all the empathy you'd like for the community, but keep boundaries, too. Otherwise, you can become such an advocate for the people you are trying to help that you can turn a blind eye to the rules and how we do things here. You can be empathetic but still maintain strong boundaries, especially if you want to keep your job."

Remember, having boundaries helps you stay clear-headed and clear-minded when making important decisions. Have empathy, but don't over-empathize so much that you lose the structure in which you must operate to keep personal integrity in your work. In other words, don't feel so sorry that you blur lines and break rules, like I did early on.

Another reason why you need to set boundaries is so that you can lead by example. Case in point, if there's a culture of low boundaries, leaders start to feel guilty when they can't attend to everyone, and this creates disorganization, chaos, and a sense of owing others when you don't. Many new community advocates are doing the work mostly from a heart place and not a head place. They are still learning and are so engrossed with what the heart feels that they have not considered what the head needs to operate and flourish. As a result, they experience burnout, intense disappointment when things don't work out, frustration, and even make questionable decisions if they don't take the full picture into account.

Boundaries are essential to survival. Do not allow your heart to trip you up. Instead, listen to that little voice in your head, too. It's important to lead with heart, but it's just as important to lead with your conscience and, specifically, your logical mind and leadership knowledge.

CHAPTER 14

Lesson #8: It's Not Written in Stone

Building a Foundation While Being Innovative and Fluid in an Ever-Changing Community

"In a world of possibility for us all, our personal visions help lay the groundwork for political action."

—AUDRE LORDE

We are working with a community and a world that is always changing. It is important that, when we are building a foundation, we understand that the foundation may need to be moved, rebuilt, or strengthened.

There's no doubt that how you respond to change will define you as a leader. Change is an ever-evolving aspect of leadership. Others look to you to be the calming force, the guidance, and the stability. Once you get comfortable with something new, something else is going to change, and you'll have to adapt. As a leader, you must stay cool in the face of change, welcome it, and find opportunities to not only adapt but grow and thrive.

CHANGE IN THE FACE OF COVID-19

When the COVID-19 pandemic hit, everything I had planned for 2020 changed. LGBTQIA+ centers set to open were paused, existing LGBTQIA+ centers were closed, community outreach events were canceled, and all in-person engagements were halted. For someone like me who created physical safe spaces with organizations, and for many of us who provided in-person services to the community, this was a game changer no one had seen before.

It pushed many of us to reimagine what we do and how we do it. We had to rethink how we show up in the world, how we create spaces, and the importance of making sure that these new safe spaces are no longer confined to physical places.

For the LGBTQIA+ centers that closed, we partnered with each other and moved all our LGBTQIA+ services and program activities online. Groups and one-on-one counseling sessions normally reserved for in-person would now be done in group and private one-on-one rooms. Highly engaging panel talks were created and shared globally versus just locally. Moving our engagement online opened the world to us. We now had people from Italy and Russia taking part in activities they would have never known about, had we never moved it online. It was during this time we realized our reach could go beyond Newark, beyond New Jersey, and even outside the USA.

It was incredibly disappointing and frustrating to not be able to open the LGBTQIA+ centers when we wanted to, and I was on a go-go-go mission! However, the downtime allowed for better deals to be made on rental spaces and site construction. It worked in the favor of some centers to wait and develop programming and plan further. Most importantly, it has enhanced the ability for many LGBTQIA+ centers to be ready if this happens again: to seize the opportunity to go beyond their local community and expand their reach.

Because I always remind myself that things can change, I

try to keep an open mind. Life happens, right? Get used to the mindset that change should pave the way for empowerment, not frustration.

As you can see, one of the challenges that I experience personally is becoming overly mission driven. Don't get so focused on only today's goals that you forget or miss out on an opportunity that could enhance or build upon your vision.

Despite COVID-19, we will continue to evolve how we do the work. I am looking at what opportunities we can create out of this pandemic to enhance our vision. How can we utilize technology to reach far beyond the walls of the city of Newark, in order to provide safe spaces in rural areas, small towns, and anywhere an internet connection can reach.

No one could have planned for the COVID-19 crisis. It caught many by surprise and struck fear into the hearts of millions. But if we shift our perspective a bit and use a little creativity, we can see the new opportunities available to us.

If you would have told me at the start of 2020 that by the end of that year, life as we know it would be moving online and all of my LGBTQIA+ centers would offer digital services only, I would have laughed in your face or had an anxiety attack. I would have never believed that in the course of a few months, we would need to transform and redefine the idea of safe spaces, the way we deliver services to the community, and the way we define LGBTQIA+ safe spaces in the world.

But you know what? We are doing it. And it's working exceptionally well on most days. Even as we are going back into the office and our LGBTQIA+ spaces, the lessons learned and benefits gained has caused us to keep our online elements in full force, enhancing our community outreach and marketing to a larger audience than before. We now have a plan B where we didn't even know we needed one. We now have a plan to stay connected and, if needed, expand our connections.

See, sometimes a mission takes little longer than planned because of a few little and sometimes big detours—like COVID-19—that will arise here and there. It is not the end of the world, and it is certainly not the end of your vision or goals. Being a successful leader requires that you regroup and create a new path to carry out the mission.

CHAPTER 15

Lesson #9: Conduct a Personal Wellness Inventory

"It is untrue that bravery can be measured by a lack of fear.
It takes guts to tremble. It takes tremble to love."

—ANDREA GIBSON

During and after a project or event, we all know the benefits of reviewing the goals that were set, what didn't work, what did, and the things we could do better next time. But very few of us apply the same attention to ourselves. It's worthwhile to take a personal inventory from time to time, self-evaluating the efforts you have poured into a project and celebrating your own successes along the way. It will also push you to investigate where you may have had good intentions with negative results so you know what to adjust in the future. It's a priceless practice to review your personal performance during a project, and to redefine your goals for the next project, to make them more achievable.

THE BENEFITS AND PROCESS OF SELF-EVALUATION

Self-evaluating during or after a project doesn't have to be a cumbersome thing. It can be something you write down and keep on hand to look back on at a later date, or it could be just a mental inventory.

These three steps will walk you through an introspective self-evaluation:

1. IDENTIFY YOUR SMART GOALS

Make note of the personal goals you set for the project. If you didn't have any specific goals, this exercise will serve as a reminder to set them next time. Remember, each goal needs to be specific, measurable, achievable, realistic, and anchored within a time frame. One of the first times I used SMART was to get my driver's permit. My SMART (specific, measurable, achievable, relevant, and time-bound) goals[24] looked something like this:

- **S:** Obtain a driver's permit.

- **M:** Get it within six months.

- **A:** Schedule a permit test time, pick up driver's manual, and study three times a week.

- **R:** Call the DMV, look up the bus schedule to visit the DMV, and schedule three days a week of study time on my phone calendar.

- **T:** Forty-five minutes for a DMV call; one hour for a DMV visit to get the manual; three days a week, I'll do one hour of study time; and schedule my permit test within six months.

Remember, keep it simple.

---

24   Mind Tools Content Team, "SMART Goals: How to Make Your Goals Achievable," *MindTools*, accessed November 23, 2021, https://www.mindtools.com/pages/article/smart-goals.htm.

2. ADDRESS THE AREAS WHERE IMPROVEMENT IS NEEDED

This is the chance for you to critique your own shortcomings. What exactly would you do differently next time? These are not failures. They are merely opportunities to learn so you don't make the same mistakes in the next project. Being aware of your weaknesses is the only way you can learn from your mistakes and grow.

3. RECORD YOUR ACCOMPLISHMENTS

Keep a running list of the tasks that you completed well, any new things that you learned, or new responsibilities you accepted. This updated list is a way to measure your growth and provide encouragement when you feel like you aren't making enough progress.

Remember, it's always okay to look back and pinpoint what may have not worked for you and adjust accordingly. Checking in on yourself can often be a difficult thing to do when we're all so busy and quick to move on to the next thing in life. However, it's important for those of us involved in community wellness to practice what we preach.

CHAPTER 16

Lesson #10: Have Something to Say

Understand the Power of Storytelling and Always Be Ready to Share Your Story

"Please remember, especially in these times of group-think
and the right-on chorus, that no person is your friend
(or kin) who demands your silence, or denies your right to grow
and be perceived as fully blossomed as you were intended."

—ALICE WALKER, NOVELIST, ESSAYIST, AND ACTIVIST

In 2010, I was a homeless constituent organizer for the Rhode Island Homeless Coalition. While in that position, I developed and led a Speaker's Bureau for displaced and former homeless community members to tell their stories in their own voices and through their lens of experience. I watched hundreds of people tell their unique stories of why and how they became homeless, and of how they have thrived, progressed, and achieved. Sharing these stories profoundly changed the misconceptions many people had for the homeless, simply by educating, creating compassion, and openly addressing stigmas.

I quickly came to understand the power of storytelling early on in my career and saw how impactful it can be to move an entire audience, create allies and partners, and motivate and inspire those in attendance. Audiences can include local business associations, hospitals, and colleges, so this was a huge opportunity to educate our community.

Like any learner, I began to buy books about storytelling and googled away. I started to interview storytellers of major Fortune 500 companies, seeking further guidance. I learned how storytelling can prove to be a leader's most powerful communication tool. It's a tool that can be used to inspire others and connect people to action.

As leaders and role models, it is integral that we are able to tell our own story before we try to speak on the larger story that represents a community. This includes addressing your trauma before attempting to deal with the community's. You should practice until you can tell your story really well. Telling your own honest and real story, both good and bad, will garner trust from the people you are working to lead and inspire. In this way, they have the motivation and confidence to go out and spread an impactful story and the urgent message you are advocating for your safe space and community.

PREPARE FOR YOUR TIME IN THE SPOTLIGHT

You can lose big opportunities to make an impact if you are not ready. When I was first given the floor or the mic, I winged it and I thought I was *that* good. But I was wrong. Afterward, I had to write that down on my self-evaluation page of my personal wellness inventory! Who was checkin' *me*, boo? Nobody. Not even myself. This is never a good idea. Remember, you can still be a badass. Just be a prepared one.

As such, when telling your personal story, preparation is key. Always have a message to share, and share it well. Practice it in front of a mirror, a friend, or a trusted co-worker for feedback. Be prepared to say something if you're ever given the opportunity, no matter the platform. From a large room full of people where they hand you a microphone, to a tiny room in a community center with three other community members, you should always be ready to share your message.

The opportunity to say something meaningful and impactful isn't always going to come with a forewarning. In other words, it won't always be a planned, prepared moment. So always keep your eyes and ears open because sometimes an opportunity will present itself, and in other cases, you in your amazingness will just create them. I often prepare my teams in this area, as they can all tell you, by giving them the mic at events. In all fairness, they know my rule about staying prepared, and I always warn them ahead of time that I'll be picking two team members to highlight their work or teams, so I'm not totally cruel.

How am I promoting the community? How am I promoting the mission? Am I giving timely information that needs to be shared? Am I providing actionable information for my audience to act on, and am I clear? These are all questions you should be asking yourself. Prepare a few stories and key points and takeaways, as well. Because you never know when you'll have the opportunity to speak and represent yourself and your cause.

An example I think of when preparing for a speaking event is when I accepted an invite to be a guest speaker for Buddies NJ, where I was asked to speak for National Latino HIV Awareness Month, and the event was themed "Changing the HIV Narrative." I prepared by learning how much time I had, who would be in the audience, professional- and community-wise. I asked about their ages and background and what message the organizations hope to leave the audience with. Sometimes this may be a call to action directly relating to the organization you are speaking for—make sure to know it way ahead of time so you can write to this direct call.

I was a little puzzled about what I would talk about until I realized, hey! I'm writing a book. So I decided I wanted to share a lesson I learned about writing an impactful story and owning the narrative. And I related it to the many HIV stories the audience members had in their pasts. My call to action was to own, write, and share those stories with the world.

Here are some things to know to prepare for speaking in public.

- **Know your audience.** Understand why they are there and what it is you wish to accomplish or communicate to the audience. Your job is to leave them with something valuable. You can only figure that out once you know who you are talking to and what motivates them.

- **Be clear, timely, and informed.** Stay on time, know your remarks, practice over and over and over again in the mirror, record yourself, and always practice in front of someone you trust for real, positive feedback.

- **Clearly communicate the call to action.** Always leave your audience with a mission or call to action. Give them the power to participate and do something by clearly communicating the need or want.

Everybody has a story to tell, but few feel comfortable sharing it, and fewer actually prepare to. Remember the best speakers in the world still get jitters even with all their preparation, so be kind to yourself and just practice. When you're ready to share, know that it takes practice and that *no one* starts off great. Yes, it matters how you *tell* your story, how you *present* your story, and *where* you do it, but what matters most is that you tell it authentically. And yes, that comes with time, too. Otherwise, the rest of us would miss out on so much learning, compassion, and connection.

STORY TRULY IS THE HUMAN ADVANTAGE

Story is what connects us to our family and family of choice, our friends, our communities, and our memories and experiences. According to Lindsay Pedersen of the *Stanford Social Innovation Review*,

> Storytelling is what unites us as humans. It connects us to one another, and it distinguishes our species from other species. Historian Yuval Noah Harari wrote in *Sapiens* of how story itself contributes to our species' competitive advantage. Our capacity to tell stories has enabled us to modify our behavior and evolve more successfully than did our peers in the animal kingdom.
>
> Through storytelling, we have been able to collaborate, persuade, lead, and follow. Storytelling puts the power into the collective, instead of into a single individual or family. This enabled us to cross barriers of time and geographical distance. We could band together to hunt big game more effectively. We could migrate in groups large enough to survive and colonize new continents that previously knew no humans. Our instinct to tell and be moved by stories enabled us to thrive, despite inferior physical strength and brain size.
>
> Cooperation is possible because of storytelling. This is the heart of brand storytelling. The promise of your business is the story of why a person should trade with you. It's the reason you are allowed to ask them for this trade.[25]

This quote reflects the importance and power behind storytelling in human history. The power to work together, build, see common goals, and take a stand against what threatens us or our

25 Lindsay Pedersen, "What's So Powerful About Storytelling?" *Stanford Social Innovation Review*, July 9, 2019, https://ssir.org/books/excerpts/entry/whats_so_powerful_about_storytelling.

existences. Stories allow us to form the bounds that we do by allowing us to see ourselves through others.

Your story matters. *You* matter. You'll gain confidence and new opportunities when you speak up. And the world will be better for having listened.

CHAPTER 17

Lesson #11: Affirmations Will Sustain and Uplift You

"It has been so important for me to embrace what I personally bring to the table. Let your stories inform your voice."

—VIVIAN NUÑEZ, FOUNDER OF TOO DAMN YOUNG

I strongly believe you don't have to be a natural-born leader to be successful. How are leaders born, anyway? The truth is, they were made: molded and nurtured through feedback, experiences, guidance, and time. If you ask me how I became a leader, I will tell you that it started with my mentors and teachers who saw something in me.

I was blessed enough to have met people who saw a purpose for my life long before I did, people who invested in my gifts and the development of my ability. Then, I had to dig my heels in and work at refining those gifts and abilities. I navigated through a lot of different and often difficult circumstances, always learning about myself and my community. Today, I can say that those journeys and experiences, no matter how difficult or painful, inform who I am now.

It's good to have an ideal reference of yourself and your values, and most importantly, you need to know what your nonnegotiables are. If you don't know what any of that is, let's sit down and figure it out together.

Some examples of nonnegotiables for my team are:

- Being a positive a role model.

- Communicating respectfully and clearly.

- Demonstrating compassion at all times.

- Doing what's right, no matter how hard.

Is your ideal version of yourself a more compassionate person? More giving? More assertive? Think about the qualities you want to have more of and less of. You need to want to fulfill that ideal self-vision as a validation of your worth. You can create daily affirmations for yourself around your vision.

CREATE YOUR OWN DAILY PERSONAL AFFIRMATIONS

I struggled with self-esteem issues my whole life. After counseling and a lot of education on mental health, I now understand that my lack of self-esteem is rooted in my early experiences in life, most notably the sexual abuse, bullying, and discrimination I suffered. I don't even think I knew the true definition of self-worth back then, even though I'd mentioned it repeatedly during my church teachings. At some point, an awareness clicked inside me. I began to truly believe what the Bible said about my purpose to the world and listened when others told me the great things they saw in me.

I've always been curious about knowledge, and I love books. One of the most instrumental books I've read on self-esteem is a book called *10 Simple Solutions for Building Self-Esteem: How to End Self-Doubt, Gain Confidence & Create a Positive Self-Image* by Glenn R. Schiraldi, PhD. Through my studies on this, I have since learned that self-esteem and self-worth are simply the level of value that you place on yourself. No one can take it away, nor can it lose value due to external life forces.

Once I began to understand that this worth is something that we are all born with, it felt possible to grow and develop it within myself. I began to educate myself more and more, and I took that new knowledge straight to the community.

Affirmations work by training your mind to focus on beliefs that empower you and build you up. One way to affirm your self-worth is by repeating daily positive affirmations. Lifehack writer Charles Sabarich has created a great list of "10 Positive Affirmations for Success That Will Change Your Life." While you're reading these ideas, be sure to come up with several of your own. Write them down in your phone, on Post-It notes around your house, or even say them out loud to yourself while getting ready each day.

1. My body is healthy; my mind is brilliant; my soul is tranquil.

2. I believe I can do anything.

3. Everything that is happening now is happening for my ultimate good.

4. I am the architect of my life; I built its foundation and choose its contents.

5. I forgive those who have harmed me in my past and peacefully detach from them.

6. My ability to conquer my challenges is limitless; my potential to succeed is infinite.

7. Today, I abandon my old habits and take up new positive ones.

8. I can achieve greatness.

9. Today, I am brimming with energy and overflowing with joy.

10. I love and accept myself for who I am.[26]

PERSONAL AFFIRMATIONS FOR LEADERSHIP

Leadership affirmations will go a long way toward enhancing your leadership abilities. And since people like to follow confident and positive people, this will help you stand out among your peers as a proven leader. For leaders, things are always changing and life can be stressful. How you approach your day, as well as the type of attitude you show up with, means a lot. These leadership affirmations can speak to the leader in you.

Repeat after me:

- I have the ability to lead and inspire others.

- My leadership qualities are evident to everyone around me. Over the years, I have developed the ability to lead a wide variety of people in any circumstance.

- I have a level of natural charisma that people find irresistible. That makes it easy for people to trust and believe in my words and my vision. People are attracted to me and what I have to say. I am a person that people follow willingly.

- It is my ability to inspire others that sets me apart.

- I know how to motivate people and present a possible future that others find fulfilling. When I inspire others,

26   Charles Sabarich, "10 Positive Affirmations for Success That Will Change your Life." *Lifehack*, November 26, 2020, https://www.lifehack.org/489003/10-positive-affirmations-for-success-that-will-change-your-life.

they can give me their best each day. When I inspire others to do their best, I am demonstrating the depth of my leadership skills.

- I am always perfecting my ability to lead and inspire. Though I already know so much, there is always more I can learn. I avoid becoming lazy and complacent. I am continuously improving my skills.

- Leadership skills are at a premium in today's world. I know that my skills are valued throughout the world.

- As my ability to lead grows, the number of opportunities available to me and to others will grow as well.

- Today, I am taking full advantage of any opportunities to lead and inspire others. I am doing my best to be a great leader as I work on strengthening my leadership skills even further.

Ask yourself:

- What opportunities do I have to be a leader in my life?

- What can I do to enhance my leadership abilities?

- What are my greatest strengths as a leader?

When you include the practice of daily affirmations into your life, it doesn't mean you will always be actively fulfilling your purpose, and it doesn't mean you won't ever behave in ways that don't necessarily reflect your ideal self. But behavior can change. When you find that you have gotten off the rails, just jump back on and get back on track. Give yourself grace and move on. Make different decisions the next time, and grow forward into the next evolution of yourself.

Quite honestly, we probably never reach our complete "ideal self." We will always be on this quest because we are always learning and growing. That's okay. You can be the most successful advocate and activist without being perfect. (I sure wasn't.) Thankfully, the two are not contingent on each other. What *is* contingent on you is your actions, your attitude, your involvement in your organization and community, and the way you present your values to the world.

Closing Thoughts

"We must be impatient for change. Let us remember that
our voice is a precious gift and we must use it."

—CLAUDIA FLORES, IMMIGRATION CAMPAIGN MANAGER,
CENTER FOR AMERICAN PROGRESS

As a young queer Latino man, I had to learn that I represented more than the gray in a black and white world. From the projects on the South Side of Newark to Little Puerto Rico in North Newark to the Gay Village in NYC, I learned fitting in is not fitting in if you're not able to express your truth, passions, and authentic self. Your voice is a powerful tool; be sure to use it or be prepared to lose it.

As you move forward in the world, I encourage you to be your unapologetic self. Allow yourself to be a student. Always seek to improve yourself and your community. Seek out mentors to nurture, guide, and provide experienced support.

Growth takes on all forms, and developing yourself is a lifelong endeavor. Remember to appreciate, pause, and slow down to enjoy all you have manifested. In the challenging moments, lean on the God of your understanding and take comfort in human resilience.

In your growth, simultaneously begin to build up others. Share your knowledge. Share your platform with those that share your passion. And don't be afraid of their potential.

Your story is important. Share it with conviction and a boldness only you can produce for the benefit and nourishment of the world.

Thank you for allowing my stories to take shelter with you, for your heart's compassion, for your mind's understanding, and most importantly, for giving me what is most precious: your time.

If you take nothing else away from this book, please know that you are sacred and by default a safe space. You are the safe space you wish to create in the world. Live and lead in your greatness.

Annual Gay Men's HIV/AIDS Awareness Day
at Rutgers University, New Brunswick, NJ (2016)

City of Newark, NJ. Credit: James R., content creator, @newarknjblog (2021)

Acknowledgments

To all the Queer Brown Boys who represent the gray in a black and white world.

Writing a book is the hardest thing I have ever done. Opening up to an audience I don't know, and sharing intimate parts of my life, is pretty terrifying. I wrestled with my own thoughts and fears. But putting this book in your hands has helped me appreciate and understand just how much I have lived, how much I have overcome, how much I have to offer my community, and how amazingly blessed I am.

This book would not have been possible if not for the incredible people I have in my life. These individuals have provided me opportunities, support, love, accountability, correction, guidance, and mentorship every single step of the way.

Thank you, Mom, for being my angel, confidante, and teacher. You are beyond selfless and giving, and I can only wish to one day display the qualities you have role-modeled for my brothers and me. Thank you for giving me the space to grow up to be my true self. Thank you for being patient and understanding, and always protecting me from the things I feared greatest in life as a kid. Thank you for blessing me with my life and those of my twin brother, Angel, and my two younger brothers, David and Jacob.

To Rafael Cuello, my partner, you have been my guiding force and the person who would push me and inspire me on the hard days. When I felt like giving up or giving in, you reminded me that there was a gay Latino boy somewhere out there looking for a story like mine in which they could see themself and understand that success and safety is within their reach. You provided the ultimate safe space to get this done. Thank you for the care you provided with each word. Thank you for our family and the love you pour on us. This could not have been done if not for you!

To Bill Orr, the founder of NJCRI and a long-standing advocate for the LGBTQIA+ community. You gave a sixteen-year-old kid an opportunity to be a part of your vision for such a fantastic organization. When it came to the nonprofit world, you showed me that lived experiences trump pedigrees of privilege, that common sense is not so common, and that providing introductions and opportunity is the price we pay for leadership and how we pay it forward.

Thishin Jackson, thank you for starting this journey with me as a brother and role model. You taught me so much at my young age. Thank you for the endless conversations after work about who we would become and what we will do for our community. Starting and growing the Project WOW LGBTQIA+ center with you is a highlighted chapter of my life. Thank you for serving our country. Until our next chapter!

Shelton Jackson, I miss you and we love you. I hope that we have helped make your vision come true. We lost you early, but I hope you know that the work we do today with our community is a result of your drive, vision, and voice at the table. Before any of us got there, you were there waiting. Rest in power, sir. Thank you.

Alex Williams, your ability to teach and pass down lived experiences through our community is priceless. You have inspired and educated countless LGBTQIA+ leaders around this country for generations to come. I am blessed to call you a friend and mentor. Your fearlessness in speaking truth to power should be witnessed by all who wish to do this work. Thank you for being an incredible source of inspiration for this book.

Tyra Gardner, thank you for always giving me the nudge to keep going. The ability to watch you grow and build your community has helped me grow. Thank you for the many panels, events, and workshops we partnered on, and for the shared energy on so many nights when we found ourselves in community centers, storefronts, and lunchrooms. You are fearless, sister.

Amistad Aromand, thank you for your mentorship and guidance in my most moldable days. You are a rock star in my eyes, and always what I would have wanted from an older brother, which you have become. You have inspired many of the pages in this book. Please continue to be you in all your essence.

Alice Sullivan, thank you for being an excellent collaborator, editor, and support. Your lessons and pep talks when I wanted to give up were invaluable to my growth in this process and, ultimately, the creation of this book today. When I first started, I knew no one in the editing or publishing world, but I came to you with an idea and you guided me along the way. Thank you for the introductions. You saved me from myself and from having some bad experiences on this journey.

Thank you to my publishing and editing team: Rikki Jump, Vi La Bianca, Mark Chait, Hal Clifford, Amy King, Charity Young, Erin Michelle Sky, Katie Villalobos, Simon Kerr, and Natalia A. Pagán Serrano.

8 Unsung LGBTQ Latinx Heroes You Should Know

by Mey Valdivia Rude[27]

June is LGBTQ Pride month, a time for us to celebrate our community, our history, our culture, and our people. We've come a long, long way since the first Pride celebrations. Latina legends, such as Sylvia Rivera and Gloria Anzaldúa, have paved the way for current Latinx LGBTQ Icons like Wilson Cruz, Sara Ramirez, and Demi Lovato.

But since Stonewall, there have been many more in the Latinx community who have made their own huge impacts on queer culture who haven't gotten proper recognition. With that in mind, we have rounded up eight of the many, many unsung LGBTQ Latinx heroes.

1. JOSÉ SARRIA

A drag queen and activist, José Sarria became the United States's first openly gay public office candidate when he ran for the San Francisco Board of Supervisors in 1961. Known as The Grand

27   Used with Mey Valdivia Rude's permission, *8 Unsung LGBTQ Latinx Heroes You Should Know*, Remezcla, https://remezcla.com/lists/culture/lgbtq-latinx-heroes/.

Mare, the Widow Norton, and Her Royal Majesty, Absolute Empress José I de San Francisco, he blazed trails as not just an openly gay man in the sixties, but a loudly and visibly gay man.

He fought against police harassment of LGBTQ people and raised awareness for gay men in San Francisco. Although he didn't win his election, he got six thousand votes, which shocked political experts and was the first evidence that the LGBTQ community could be a formidable voting bloc.

2. DENNIS DELEON

In 1993, Dennis deLeon publicly disclosed his HIV status in an op-ed for *The New York Times*, becoming one of the first New York City officials to do so. He was a dedicated HIV/AIDS activist and Latino community leader who served as both the New York City Human Rights Commissioner and President of the Latino Commission on AIDS. Under his tenure as president, the organization grew from a small local organization with a staff of just two into a national organization with forty-five employees and a $5 million budget. It did work to translate AIDS information into Spanish, built networks of Spanish-language AIDS prevention programs, and raised awareness of AIDS in the Latino community. He was diagnosed with HIV in 1986 and lived until 2009 when he passed away at the age of sixty-one.

3. HORACIO ROQUE RAMÍREZ

Horacio Roque Ramírez was a Salvadoran-American writer, advocate, and oral historian who focused his work on LGTBQ Latinos and specifically the experiences of Central American Latinos. At the time of his death, Ramírez was working on a book of oral history about Latino communities in San Francisco. He was one of the first historians to study and chronicle the lives of gay Latinos in the Mission District.

4. GIL CUADROS

Gil Cuadros was a Chicano poet in the nineties. He's one of the few gay Latinos publicly talking about HIV/AIDS and its effect on the community. After his partner died and he was diagnosed with AIDS in 1987, Cuadros took a writing workshop for people with HIV and began a journey of writing about his community that would last for the final eight years of his life. His works are believed to be the first chronicles of what life was like for Chicanos with AIDS. His book, *City of God*, is full of short stories and poems that deal with the experiences of queer Chicanos and, especially, queer Chicanos with AIDS. He was also one of the early chroniclers of the queer community in Los Angeles.

5. RANE ARROYO

Rane Arroyo was an openly gay Puerto Rican poet, playwright, and scholar who wrote extensively on immigration, Latino culture in the United States, and homosexuality. Many of his works were autobiographical and dealt with his life as a gay Puerto Rican. He published eleven books of poetry and won numerous awards for his groundbreaking writing on the gay Puerto Rican experience, including the Carl Sandburg Poetry Prize. His poetry is included in the *Heath Anthology of American Literature*, one of the most commonly taught books in US English college classes.

6. JEANNE CÓRDOVA

Córdova, who was born in Germany to a Mexican father and Irish-American mother, became one of the most influential lesbian activists in American history during her forty-year career as an activist, community organizer, and journalist. She served as the Los Angeles chapter president of the early lesbian rights group Daughters of Bilitis and opened the first lesbian center in the city. She also headed up her chapter's newsletter, which she helped become *The Lesbian Tide*, the first American magazine with "lesbian" in the title and one of the most respected queer publications of its time.

She was a key organizer in many of the first lesbian and women's conferences, and worked to fight against anti-LGBT laws in California. She spent the next several decades continuing this work and blazing new paths for lesbians and wrote an award-winning memoir, *When We Were Outlaws: A Memoir of Love and Revolution*.

7. WILLIAM BRANDON LACY CAMPOS

William Brandon Lacy Campos started his activism when he was just a teen, joining several queer student groups and co-chairing the United States Student Association's Queer Student Coalition. He also spoke frequently about his HIV-positive status and the issues that HIV-positive men of color face. Before passing away in 2012, William served as the co-executive director of Queers for Economic Justice and was a board member of the Audre Lorde Project. He also served as a spokesman for an HIV-positive dating site.

8. ANGIE XTRAVAGANZA

For many queer Latinxs in New York, the ballroom scene is where they found their family and where they were able to express themselves. That is, in large part, due to Angie Xtravaganza, who became House Mother of the primarily Latinx ball house, The House of Xtravaganza. Xtravaganza and her house were featured in the groundbreaking documentary *Paris is Burning*, and under her tutelage, the house produced a number of ballroom and dance legends, like Venus Xtravaganza and Madonna's "Vogue" choreographers Jose Gutierez and Luis Camacho. She is remembered as one of the great house mothers in all of ball culture.

8 Pioneering Trans Latinas to Honor During Women's History Month

by Mey Valdivia Rude[28]

Women's History Month is a hugely important time of year when we highlight the contributions women have made and continue to make to history. But as we acknowledge and celebrate how they broke barriers and pushed society forward, it's crucial we don't just talk about one type of woman. We need to learn about how women of different races, ethnicities, backgrounds, and nationalities have shaped our lives. That's why we're looking at trans Latinas currently making their mark within both LGBTQ communities and overall. These women, like Sylvia Rivera and Angie Xtravaganza before them, are currently building lasting legacies. For the most part, their work goes unrecognized, but they deserve to be a part of the conversation as well.

Here are eight trans Latinas we can't forget as we observe Women's History Month.

---

28   Used with Mey Valdivia Rude's permission, "8 Pioneering Trans Latinas to Honor During Women's History Month," *Remezcla*, https://remezcla.com/lists/culture/trans-latinas-to-celebrate-during-womens-history-month/, 03/12/2018.

1. JENNICET GUTIÉRREZ

Many people first heard of Jennicet Gutiérrez when she interrupted former President Barack Obama to demand accountability for his actions on immigration. But she's also been doing good and hard work for trans women and immigrants for years. The Mexico-born activist is one of the founding members of La Familia: Trans Queer Liberation Movement, which "works at local and national levels to achieve the collective liberation of trans, queer, and gender-nonconforming Latinxs through building community, organizing, advocacy, and education." Much of her work focuses on trans and other LGBTQ Latinx caught up in the immigration system. She works so that undocumented trans women can be free, safe, and successful in the United States.

2. LEIOMY MALDONADO

Leiomy Maldonado is one of the Queens of the Ballroom scene and a true legend. This Puerto Rican trans woman is known as the "Wonder Woman of Vogue" for the way she's revolutionized and led the LGBTQ dance and ballroom community. She appeared as part of the Vogue Evolution dance crew on MTV's *America's Best Dance Crew*. From there, she's gone on to choreograph and star in music videos, such as Willow Smith's "Whip My Hair" and Icona Pop's "All Night." Most recently, she starred in a Nike #BeTrue TV ad in support of Pride Month. The commercial made her the first trans woman to star in a Nike ad.

3. RUBY CORADO

Salvadoran activist Ruby Corado founded the Washington, DC-based Casa Ruby, a bilingual, multicultural LGBT organization. Casa Ruby's mission is to make "success life stories among transgender, genderqueer, and gender-nonconforming Gay,

Lesbian, and Bisexual people." Casa Ruby offers support groups, housing referrals and case management, legal services, hot meals, clothing exchange, and more to some of the LGBT community's most vulnerable members. She also fought to make the Washington, DC, Human Rights Act cover protections for gender identity and expression. She's won many awards for her service.

4. BAMBY SALCEDO

As the founder of the TransLatin@ Coalition in Los Angeles, Mexico-born Bamby Salcedo not only advocates for the needs of trans Latinxs who have immigrated to the United States, but also speaks about and fights for the rights and safety of those living with HIV and AIDS. In 2016, the Obama Administration invited her to speak at the White House United State of Women Summit, where she spoke out about ways to help prevent violence against women. She continues to speak and work with LGBTQ Latinxs and win awards for her advocacy and community work.

5. MARIAH LOPEZ

Mariah Lopez is a former sex worker who now serves as the executive director for the Strategic Trans Alliance for Radical Reform (STARR). In 2006, she was arrested for "loitering with intent for solicitation" in New York City. Police officers and prison workers abused her and ordered her to undergo a "genital check" before allowing her into a women's prison. When she refused, they placed her in a men's prison, where she repeatedly faced sexual harassment and assault by both inmates and officers. Since then, she's fought hard to make sure that transgender inmates have safe facilities in prison, where they're protected from that kind of abuse. She also speaks and advocates for LGBTQ people of color with low incomes.

6. DIANE MARIE RODRÍGUEZ ZAMBRANO

Diane Marie Rodríguez Zambrano is an Ecuadorian activist who, in 2013, became the first openly trans or even LGBT candidate to run for office in her home country. She's fought to include the rights of trans people in the workplace, so that employers will respect their gender identity and name changing rights. She's also worked to end discrimination and stigmas against LGBT people in Ecuador. She continues to fight today and work with the government in order to improve life for trans Ecuadorians.

7. VICTORIA CRUZ

Victoria Cruz, a contemporary of famous trans activists like Marsha P. Johnson and Sylvia Rivera, continues fights for trans and women's rights. At age four, she moved from Puerto Rico to Brooklyn and transitioned at a young age. In the nineties, she started a long career helping LGBT people who have been victims of violence and rape when she joined the Anti-Violence Project. She worked as a domestic violence counselor and received an award from Attorney General Eric Holder in 2012 for her service to victims of violent crimes.

8. FELICIA ELIZONDO

Felicia Elizondo is an HIV-positive activist and speaker who has actively fought for LGBT rights since the 1960s when she participated in Compton's Cafeteria Riots, which preceded the famous Stonewall Riots. Since then, she's also worked with the San Francisco AIDS Foundation, the Shanti Project, and other organizations that improve the lives of people with serious illnesses. Apart from her HIV/AIDS activism, she's also worked with other trans women of color to fight racism. She was named

the Lifetime Achievement Grand Marshal of the 2015 San
Francisco Pride Parade.

Helpful LGBTQIA+ Resources

If you or someone you know has been sexually assaulted, here are some LGBTQ-friendly resources listed below:

- National Sexual Assault Hotline: they can also refer you to a local rape crisis center. Call 1-800-656-HOPE (4673) 24/7 or Online Counseling at https://ohl.rainn. org/online/.

- Loveisrespect Hotline: 1-866-331-9474 (24/7) or Text "loveis" to 22522.

- The Anti-Violence Project serves people who are LGBTQIA+. Hotline: 212-714-1124, bilingual 24/7.

- LGBT National Help Center: National Hotline, 1-888-843-4564, or National Youth Talkline, 1-800-246-7743.

- Online Peer Support Chat: https://www.glbthotline.org/peer-chat.html or Weekly Youth Chatrooms at https://www.glbthotline.org/youthchatrooms.html.

- National Domestic Violence Hotline: 1-800-799-7233 or text START to 88788.

- FORGE serves transgender and gender-nonconforming survivors of domestic and sexual violence; provides referrals to local counselors. Call 414-559-2123.

- The Network la Red serves LGBTQ, poly, and kink/BDSM survivors of abuse; bilingual. Hotline: 617-742-4911.

- Northwest Network serves LGBT survivors of abuse; can provide local referrals. Call their hotline at 206-568-7777.

About the Author

"Blood does not make family. Those are relatives. Family is
those with whom you share your good, bad, and ugly, and still love
one another in the end. Those are the ones you select."

—HECTOR XTRAVAGANZA, HOUSE OF XTRAVAGANZA

At the age of sixteen, Safe Space Expert and LGBTQIA+ Rights
Advocate, Julio C. Roman, accepted his calling in LGBTQIA+
activism and safe space design.

Julio has dedicated over twenty-two years to creating
LGBTQIA+ safe spaces and advancing the health equality and
social justice initiatives of Black and Brown Lesbian, Gay, Bisexual,
and Transgender communities, and other marginalized communities affected by HIV/AIDS and its related health, social, and
economic disparities.

His experience lies extensively in Safe Space Design, HIV
Prevention and Harm Reduction Programming, Community
Engagement, LGBTQIA+ Advocacy, Leadership Development,
and LGBTQIA+ Organizational Development. He has a passion
for mentoring, building highly effective teams, and working with
other amazing change agents in and outside of the LGBTQIA+
social movement. He champions the idea that "highly effective leaders, coupled with highly engaging and inspirational

LGBTQIA+ Empowerment Centers and safe spaces, save lives and create other leaders."

Julio is a founding member and co-founder of two LGBTQIA+ centers in the city of Newark. He often presents and publishes his public health findings on local, state, and national levels. He has been honored to represent the LGBTQIA+ community on Capitol Hill DC, State Department DC, World Monetary Fund DC, and the United Nations NYC. And continues to be featured in *Insider NJ's* "Out 100: The LGBT Power List" for his leadership in community organizing and HIV/AIDS work.

He currently serves on the Board of Directors at ARK of Freedom Alliance, a national anti-human trafficking organization, and proudly serves as an LGBTQIA+ Commissioner for Newark, New Jersey. He continues to work with LGBTQIA+ organizations nationally.

Julio resides in Newark with his partner and two four-legged children, the Duke and Duchess of Forest Hills.

For the latest information, or to contact Julio, please visit www.juliocroman.com.

Made in the USA
Middletown, DE
03 June 2022